Distinctive Details

from *Threads*

Distinctive Details

Great Embellishment Techniques for Clothing

from *Threads*

The Taunton Press

Taunton
BOOKS & VIDEOS
for fellow enthusiasts

First printing: January 1995
Second printing: December 1995
Printed in the United States of America

A THREADS Book

THREADS® is a trademark of The Taunton Press, Inc.,
registered in the U.S. Patent and Trademark Office.

The Taunton Press
63 South Main Street
Box 5506
Newtown, CT 06470-5506

Library of Congress Cataloging-in-Publication Data

Distinctive details : great embellishment techniques for clothing /
    from Threads.
        p.   cm.
    "A Threads book" — T.p. verso.
    Includes index.
    ISBN 1-56158-095-3
    1. Fancy work. 2. Clothing and dress. I. Threads magazine.
TT750.D58   1995   94-37377
    746.9'2 — dc20   CIP

Contents

Introduction

Whether your next special project is a tailored jacket, a sensational party dress or simply a vest that's fun to wear, you'll want it to be your personal creation. And what better way to do that than to go beyond the pattern and add an elegant detail or touch of whimsy? From buttons to beads, from one-of-a-kind closures to couture quilting, from luxurious lace to leaf printing, here is a repertoire of embellishment techniques you can use to personalize all your clothing.

Distinctive Details is a valuable resource of innovative ideas from sewing experts and fashion professionals. You'll share in their design processes, find step-by-step instructions to duplicate their techniques and get encouragement to take an idea one step further.

So join thousands of readers of *Threads* magazine and let your imagination work with you at your machine. You'll love the results.

Suzanne LaRosa, publisher

Elegant, Functional Bindings

In Jeanne Marc garments, bindings finish and embellish seams and edges

by Claire B. Shaeffer

Every seam and edge is an opportunity for embellishment: From Jeanne Marc's Spring '94 collection, this ruched jacket has bindings added to all its edges including the front zipper placket and armscye seams.

*f*or the San Francisco design firm Jeanne Marc, ordinary construction details like seams and zipper plackets are not just functional elements of a garment. They're opportunities for embellishment.

Jeanne Marc designs are colorful, whimsically sophisticated, and recognizable in part by their signature use of construction details as trim. Created by the husband-and-wife team of Marc Grant and Jeanne Allen, these designs are intended for the customer who wants something different but not trendy. While bindings are by no means the only embellishment found on these garments, they're my favorite because they're versatile and offer rich possibilities for unusual designs. In this article you'll find my home sewers' adaptation of this firm's binding techniques.

At Jeanne Marc, bindings are often made of contrasting fabrics to define and accentuate a garment's edges or seams or to transform a utilitarian zipper placket, practical button loop, or plain sleeve cuff into dramatic details. (For a subtler effect, you could, of course, make the bindings of self-fabric.) The finished bindings on these garments can be narrow (¼ in.) or wide (⅞ in.) and used alone or paired with a second, narrower binding or a small piping. The binding itself is sometimes left plain and at other times embellished with decorative serged stitches. When the binding covers a seam whose allowances have been turned to the right side of the garment, the bound seam can either stand boldly upright or be stitched flat against the fabric. Turning the allowances to the right side offers an added bonus for an unlined garment: a neat plain seam on the inside of the garment.

Keys to success
Applying binding successfully results from several key factors, according to Jeanne Allen: stiffening the binding fabric to make it easier to work with and to prevent any wrinkling, carefully cutting the binding fabric, and shaping the edge or seam that's being bound.

Stiffening binding fabric—Jeanne Marc starches *all* its binding fabrics, from cottons to rayons and polyesters, before cutting them. (Although the firm doesn't design with wools, these too could be stiffened with starch or with a light interfacing like Touch o' Gold.) The staff dip 5- to 15-yd. pieces into liquid starch, then carefully smooth them over wooden poles and allow them to air dry before

sending them out to be cut into strips and made into rolls of unfolded bias. Since you won't need such a large piece of fabric, you can prepare yours at home using liquid starch from the grocery store and the shower rod as a drying rack. Or, if you want to make your bias strips from small fabric scraps, you can use spray starch.

Cutting binding fabric—Always cut binding fabric on the bias since it's easier to shape than fabric cut on the crosswise or lengthwise grain. Almost any fabric can be bound, but use only light- to medium-weight fabrics for the bindings themselves. Heavier-weight fabrics will be too bulky for clean, attractive bindings.

Always cut the binding strip wide enough to wrap easily around the edges or seams you're binding. For bindings made of crisp, lightweight fabrics like cotton broadcloth and linen, cut the unfolded fabric twice the width of the finished binding plus ½ to ⅝ in. total for seam allowances. For soft fabrics like rayon and slippery ones like polyester, cut the strip twice the width of the finished binding plus ⅝ to ¾ in. so that you'll be better able to fold under and control the seam allowances. Do likewise for medium-weight fabrics like midwale corduroy (11 to 15 wales per in.); add ⅝ to ¾ in. to the

basic measurement since more fabric will be taken up in the folds.

At Jeanne Marc, the binding is folded as it's applied with a special industrial binder attachment. You can fold and press your bias strips with a cardboard template or with a bias tape maker (available at your local fabric store). Both work well, but a template offers more flexibility for fine-tuning a binding's width and narrowing the seam allowances when reducing bulk is important.

To determine the best width for the unfolded bias, make a few samples. To do so, cut several bias strips in different widths. If you're binding a somewhat bulky edge comprised of several layers, it's a good idea to mock up the edge to test your binding samples. Follow the directions on p. 10 to prepare your bias strips and make your test bindings.

If the edge you're binding is a single layer but made of heavyweight, bulky, or quilted fabric, you may find the sample binding a little bulky and unattractive. In this case, trim away some of the seam allowance or pull out a little batting from the quilted edge to reduce bulk, and then make another sample. (Don't trim the interfacing or seam allowances on edges made of light- to medium-weight fabrics since they support the edge and help it hold its shape.) ⇨

Enhancing a decorative binding: In this detail of the jacket shown on the facing page, a simple binding is embellished with serged stitches in gold thread.

Shaping edges or seams being bound—
No less important than the cut of the binding itself is the cut shape of the edge or seam being bound. A straight edge or seam presents little problem, but a curved one can be tricky to bind smoothly. If the curve is too sharp, the binding may ripple when applied. To prevent this, gently round a curved edge before binding it.

Be careful when reshaping a curved neckline. It may seem logical to enlarge the curve by trimming it evenly, but this produces a neckline that's unbecoming and won't sit well on the body. Instead, take off about ¼ in. at the back neck, ½ in. at the shoulders, and 1 in. or more at the front neck. Before cutting the neckline larger, make one or more paper patterns to hold up and try different necklines to find the one that's most attractive for you.

Since it's faster to bind a curve than a corner, Jeanne Marc designs usually don't have square corners. Instead, the staff sometimes add a faced band along an edge and bind the curved seam joining the band to the garment (photo on p. 12). If you want to bind a square corner, you'll find directions at right, but note that it will tend to curl more than a bound curve.

Binding an edge

A bound edge is usually slightly crisper and has less drape than one that's hemmed or faced. It also has a little more weight and will cause the edge to droop or collapse if not supported appropriately. At Jeanne Marc, an edge is both interfaced and faced before being bound. If the designers are making a garment from a soft fabric like polyester, they'll alter the design to add a band at the edge, which enables them to interface the band and keep the soft edge from appearing overwhelmed by the facing. The general binding sequence is shown at right.

Interfacing a facing—After cutting binding strips and pressing under the seam allowances, prepare the edge for binding. Use the facing pattern to cut interfacing for the edge and, if you're adding a band to the edge, use the garment pattern to cut additional interfacing. Fuse the interfacings to the wrong side of the garment sections and assemble facing and garment sections. With wrong sides together, pin the facing to the garment. Stitch a scant ¼ in. from the edge and press the edge flat.

Applying a binding to a curved edge—
To apply a partially folded binding, first fold it in half lengthwise with wrong sides together, and finger-press it. Then carefully cover the garment edge and pin the binding in place so it's neither tight

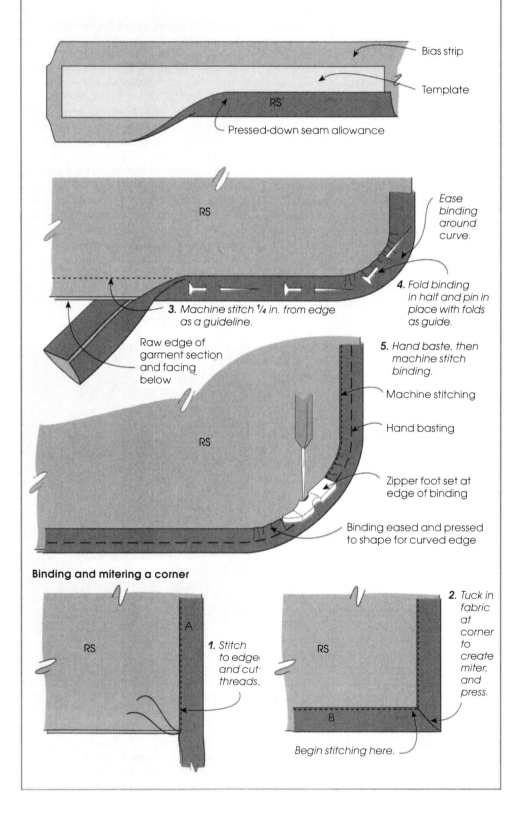

Basic technique for binding an edge

Preparing binding strips: Unless carefully measured, cut, and folded, bias binding strips will ripple when applied.

1. After starching fabric, cut strips on true bias (see Threads No. 51, pp. 50-53), measuring twice binding's finished width plus ½ to ⅝ in. total for seam allowance (or ⅝ to ¾ in. for bulky or slippery fabrics).

2. Make template twice binding's finished width (add ⅛ in. extra for bulky fabrics), and center on binding strip. Iron seam allowances over template.

Bias strip

Template

Pressed-down seam allowance

RS

RS

Ease binding around curve.

3. Machine stitch ¼ in. from edge as a guideline.

Raw edge of garment section and facing below

4. Fold binding in half and pin in place with folds as guide.

5. Hand baste, then machine stitch binding.

Machine stitching

Hand basting

RS

Zipper foot set at edge of binding

Binding eased and pressed to shape for curved edge

Binding and mitering a corner

RS

A

1. Stitch to edge and cut threads.

Begin stitching here.

RS

B

2. Tuck in fabric at corner to create miter, and press.

Piping a binding

Piping is a subtle embellishment that, when worked in a contrasting fabric, adds a wonderful hint of color to a binding. To keep the binding supple, add piping to the edge rather than to the binding itself. Attach piping with stitching ¼ in. from garment edge. Apply the binding as shown at right and below, with folds on stitching.

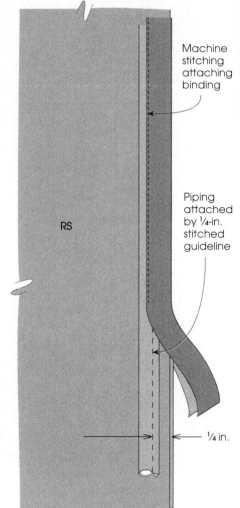

RS

Machine stitching attaching binding

Piping attached by ¼-in. stitched guideline

¼ in.

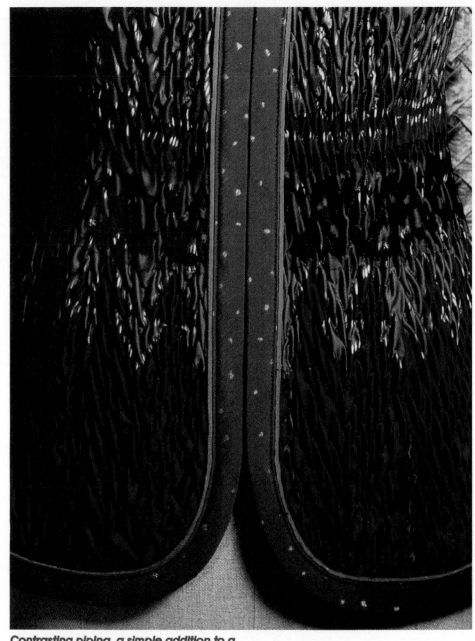

Contrasting piping, a simple addition to a binding, provides a lively hint of color.

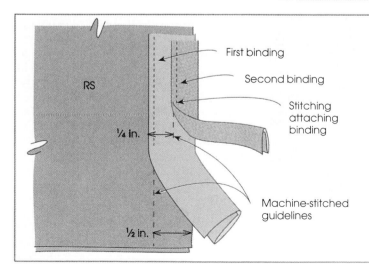

RS

First binding

Second binding

Stitching attaching binding

¼ in.

Machine-stitched guidelines

½ in.

Making a double binding

A double binding is nothing more than a narrow binding applied on top of a wide one.

1. Apply wider binding first as you would a single binding, using the directions on the facing page, with one exception: Stitch the guideline for first binding placement ½ in. rather than ¼ in. from garment edge.

2. Stitch a guideline ¼ in. from outer edge of first binding and apply second binding.

Avoid binding corners by adding a faced band around the garment edge. On this jacket, a white binding covers the seam joining the black band to the garment.

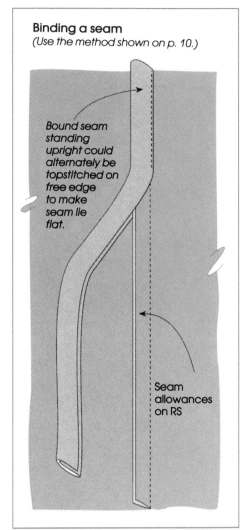

Binding a seam
(Use the method shown on p. 10.)

Bound seam standing upright could alternately be topstitched on free edge to make seam lie flat.

Seam allowances on RS

nor loose and its edges barely cover the ¼-in. stitching line, as shown on p. 10.

For an outward curve, ease and pin the binding so its outer folded edge isn't so tight that it cups under. For an inward curve, pull the binding taut to make the folded edge lie flat.

Carefully hand baste the binding in place, catching its edges on both sides of the garment. Press lightly and, at the curves, press and shrink the excess binding. Machine stitch the binding, using the zipper foot set to ride on the binding (another foot would have to straddle the different heights of the binding and edge). Remove bastings and press again.

Binding a corner with mitered bias—
This is a two-step process, as shown in the bottom drawing sequence on p. 10. To bind a mitered corner rather than a curve, pin, baste, and stitch the binding the full

Using bindings at closures

Bindings can be decoratively incorporated into closures or can become actual closures. On a zippered edge, the binding hides the closure. For a button loop, the binding extends beyond the edge of the garment.

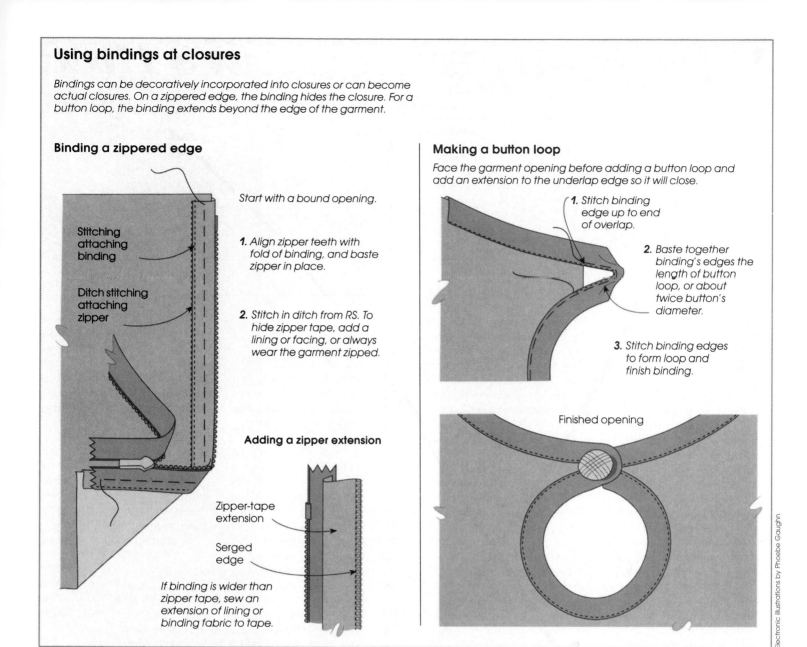

Binding a zippered edge

Stitching attaching binding

Ditch stitching attaching zipper

Start with a bound opening.

1. Align zipper teeth with fold of binding, and baste zipper in place.

2. Stitch in ditch from RS. To hide zipper tape, add a lining or facing, or always wear the garment zipped.

Adding a zipper extension

Zipper-tape extension

Serged edge

If binding is wider than zipper tape, sew an extension of lining or binding fabric to tape.

Making a button loop

Face the garment opening before adding a button loop and add an extension to the underlap edge so it will close.

1. Stitch binding edge up to end of overlap.

2. Baste together binding's edges the length of button loop, or about twice button's diameter.

3. Stitch binding edges to form loop and finish binding.

Finished opening

length of one side of the corner and cut the threads before pinning and basting the second side. Pull the binding up to the second side, then tuck under the triangles of fabric at the corner, front and back, to create a miter; press the miter flat. Pin and baste the second side. Begin machine stitching the edge at the miter with a spot tack (several stitches taken in place) to lock the stitching. Remove the bastings and press.

Binding a seam

To bind a seam, first sew the seam with wrong sides together, so the allowances appear on the right side of the garment. Then bind the allowances using the directions for binding an edge on p. 10.

For a bold design, leave the bound seam upright (see the drawing on the facing page). For a flatter, more subtle finish, press the binding to one side and stitch along its folded edge through all the layers to make it lie flat against the garment.

When a bound upright seam is to be crossed by another seam or binding, fold and pin the upright seam away from the garment center when it's on the garment front or back or toward the back when it's on the shoulder or under the arm.

Finishing the ends of a binding—When a binding and seam intersect, finishing a binding's ends is easy since they can be tucked into the seamline. If you're binding the edges of a garment that opens down the front, leave the left side seams open on both the garment and the facing until after applying the binding. By beginning the binding at the left side seam, you'll bind the front of the garment first and the back hem last so that any cumulative shifting that occurs in the binding's bottom layer will be minimal on the

garment front. After applying the binding, tuck its ends into the side seam, and complete the seam.

If the binding on your design doesn't intersect a seam, you can finish the ends by lapping one over the other. Try to position the lapped finish at an inconspicuous place (this means planning ahead where to start and finish the binding). To lap the ends, cut the finishing end of the binding fabric on the diagonal (which is the straight grain) and turn it under ¼ in. Then lap this folded edge ¼ in. over the beginning end of the binding and finish machine stitching the binding. And with that, you've finished your binding. □

Claire B. Shaeffer is the author of Couture Sewing Techniques, *published by The Taunton Press (1994). She teaches couture sewing techniques at the College of the Desert in Palm Desert, CA.*

Sheer Magic

Layering transparent fabrics over other textiles creates multiple options for new surfaces

by Lois Ericson

Unless you specialize in them, you've probably considered the sheer fabrics in your yardage store's bridal department to be out of your area of interest. But wait until you start exploring the amazing effects you can achieve by layering sheer fabrics over all types of other fabrics. My local store's sheer department hasn't been safe since I discovered how dramatically, yet with so little effort, I can transform, enhance, soften, and modify every other fabric in my collection, simply by laying a sheer on top. You can even use sheers to protect fragile textiles, antiques, beadwork, loose pieces, and yarn collages, making it possible to sew wearable garments with them.

One of the most inviting aspects of layering sheers is that you don't have to change your sewing plans in any way in order to use the new fabrics you've created. I simply machine baste, pin, or tack the sheer layer to the base fabric for easy handling, either along an edge or two, or by machine embroidering over the layers in a few places for a decorative effect. The additional layer(s) add so little bulk that I can almost always proceed using the same construction techniques that I would have used with the base fabric before layering.

A sheers catalog

Theatrical and costume supply houses probably offer the widest selection of sheer fabrics and have the most unusual offerings, but stores that feature lots of designer fabrics are good sources for sheers, as well. I check the Yellow Pages for such stores when I visit a large city. The larger mail-order fabric houses all have good collections of sheers. Following is a list of the choices you'll have in a typical fabric store's sheer department.

Organza: A crisp, matte finish silk. Also made from rayon or poly, which can have a sheen. Iridescent and metallic are available. Silk organza, in all variations, is the sheer I use most; its crispness keeps large areas in place with a minimum of stitches.

Chiffon: Available in silk and synthetics and in many colors; very soft, and drapes well. You can make chiffon more crisp and easier to handle by spray-starching it before sewing and between cleanings.

Georgette: Silk or rayon crepe, similar to chiffon. Highly twisted yarns give it a slightly rough texture.

Voile: Usually cotton, also sometimes in silk; crisp, but less so than organza.

Batiste: Soft cotton, and poly/cotton; comes in a wide range of colors, but it's not as transparent as other sheers.

Net: Usually nylon or poly, available in various sizes and many colors; large mesh net is called mosquito netting.

Tulle: Usually nylon or poly; a fine net with a hexagonal pattern, limited colors, quite fragile.

On the next few pages you'll find a gallery of sheer-layering experiments that merely hint at the possibilities. ⇨

Lois Ericson's latest book, What Goes Around, *is about belts. It is available from her at PO Box 5222, Salem, OR 97304.*

A coat made from sheers? Look closely and you'll see sheer strips and ribbons collaged beneath the hand-painted organza of the orange panels. The accent fabric is also a composite, proving that sheers needn't look sheer.

Changing colors and unifying designs:

The simplest application of layered sheers is just to change the color of a fabric by putting a transparent layer over it (photo above). Try white or black sheers to lighten or darken without changing the color of the underlayer. The pattern or design of the underlayer will be softened or muted, and any strong contrasts in the design will be brought into greater harmony.

A sheer layer can instantly unify a fabric collage composition that's getting out of hand, while holding it together physically. You don't even have to finish the raw edges underneath—you can simply fuse or tack the pieces in position. You can include delicate elements like strands of unstitched metallic thread, loose yarn, and other decorative scraps, textile-based or not. Adding multiple sheer layers, either all over or selectively, allows you to increase the muting effect, or even create opacity, exactly where you want it. You can collage small sheer pieces under the top layer, or create layered stripes by tucking or pleating the top layer.

Moiré effects:

If you experiment with shifting multiple layers of organza (and some other sheers), you can create fascinating moiré effects, as in the garment below. This multilayered vest started with reverse-appliquéd lozenges of magenta pinstripes on a muslin-colored ground, covered with large scraps of black organza and loose magenta threads, all held in place with an overlayer of more black organza. Lois Ericson has even used two layers of organza sewn together as a fashion fabric—the subtle movement of the moiré may be all the embellishment you need. ⇨

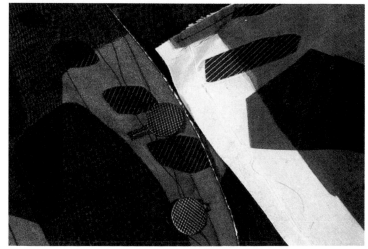

Layering prints:
If you want to intensify a dull base fabric, consider a patterned overlay. Many sheers are available in prints, which can combine dramatically with bold, graphic prints or striped base fabric, as you can see in the detail of the belt above. You can create similar results to order by painting patterns on plain sheers with fabric paints. Many sheers are also embroidered, sequined, or otherwise combined with opaque, textured areas. These can add impact to subtle underlayer designs, as shown in the widely different effects in the photo at left, in which a metallic-embroidered sheer is layered over matching red tussah, ethnic woven patterns, and crinkled satin.

Sheers for protection: *Using sheers to protect fragile underlayer textiles offers unlimited possibilities, especially if muting the underlayer pattern suits your design (see photo below). Raveling fabrics, brocade floats, feathers, lace, passementerie, and the like can all be used in sturdy, wearable garments. Color-matched netting allows you to layer fragile treasures almost invisibly. The vest at right was made from fragments of an old beaded garment that Lois Ericson first permanently basted to tailors' felt to form a firm backing. To protect the beading, she placed two layers of black nylon netting over all, which she tacked in place by hand in various places. Contrasting nets and tulle are also wonderful for creating subtle shading effects, without completely changing the base fabric.*

(Ed. note: If you're inspired by this article to create something you're pleased with, please let us know!)

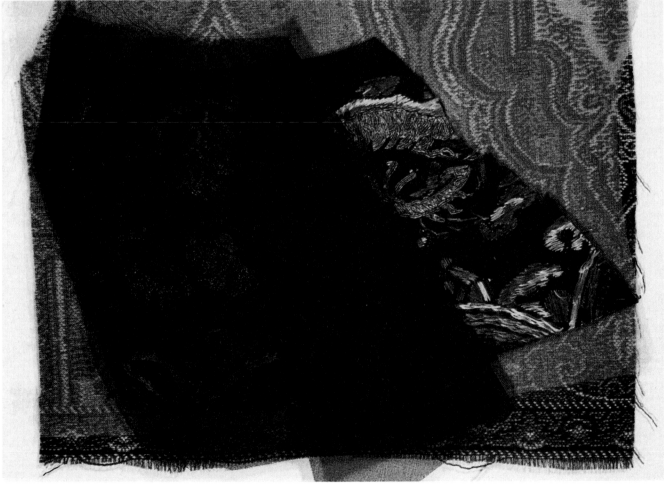

Now You See It, Now You Don't

Soluble stabilizers revolutionize machine embroidery

by Cindy Hickok

the idea is simple: Embroider directly onto a soluble fabric, then dip the piece in water and watch the background disappear like magic, leaving only the embroidery. The material that makes this possible, a space-age product of polyvinyl alcohol (PVA) fibers, was originally made for the garment industry. As an artist, I find it a fascinating new tool for creating both free-standing works and embellished garments.

Water-soluble material can be used as a stabilizer with other fabrics, or as a fabric in its own right. Placed over a textured or pile fabric, the stabilizer prevents embroidery from disappearing in the pile. It also keeps presser feet from catching in pile loops, a real aid in monogramming towels. Industrial appliquérs use soluble material over the appliqué shapes to hold them in place for stitching without curling at the edges. By itself, water-soluble fabric allows you to make free-motion embroidery motifs and lace edging as shown in the photo at left.

A choice of fabrics

Soluble fabrics fall into two categories: those that dissolve in cold water, and those that require hot (simmering) water. I prefer the

Make embellishments like openwork petals (at left) using free-motion embroidery and water-soluble fabric. (Photo by Susan Kahn)

hot-water material because of its durability, but there are advantages and disadvantages to each. Neither product is expensive, but the hot-water fabric sells for slightly more than the cold. Both fabrics should be stored in a cool, dry place; manufacturers discourage long-term storage in plastic bags.

Cold-water-soluble material, which is colorless and resembles a plastic food-storage bag, is available in many fabric stores, sold either by the yard or precut and packaged, labeled as water-soluble plastic stabilizers; brand names include Aqua-Film, Aquasolve, Hiselon, and Solvy. Nancy's Notions (800-765-0690) sells it as Wash-Away Plastic Stabilizer. Use cold-water-soluble stabilizer for delicate fabrics or designs that need careful handling during the dissolving process, such as the lace edging shown in the series of photos at right. You can pin a delicate piece to a padded surface and then gently immerse it, padding and all, in cold water. With the cold-water-soluble fabric, you can use shiny threads and metallics that do not stand up to harsh treatment and hot temperatures, but the fabric will stretch when subjected to heavy stitching.

Hot-water-soluble fabric, sold under the brand name Solvron, is light blue, and looks and feels like organza. It's easy to draw on and won't tear or stretch easily when heavily stitched. Because Solvron must be immersed in simmering water, it is less suitable for delicate threads or fabrics. Solvron shrinks somewhat during dissolving, so it may pucker the garment if used to make edgings or insets in other fabrics. It is best used for embroidery alone, which can be carefully stretched back to its original size as it dries. For information on purchasing hot-water-soluble fabric, send a stamped, self-addressed envelope to: Water Soluble Fabric, 523 Briar Path, Houston, TX 77079. Outside the U.S., contact Madeira Threads (UK) Ltd., Thirsk Industrial Park, York Road, Thirsk, North Yorkshire YO7 3BX, England.

At the time of this writing, Madeira is beginning to import a third type of water-soluble fabric which combines cold-water solubility with the stability of Solvron. While I've not had the chance to test it, it may be the best of both worlds.

Using the materials

I work intricate miniature embroidery designs onto soluble fabric, and after dissolving the background, mount them for display. After carefully planning the pieces, I transfer the design to the soluble fabric before beginning the machine stitching.

I use a wooden hoop tightened by a spring or screw. Make sure the hoop you choose has no rough edges and will fit easily under your machine needle; many craft-shop hoops are too wide. Choose a diameter you

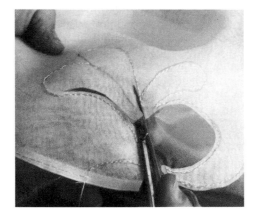

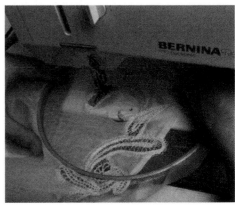

Combining fabrics and openwork embroidery: To make a decorative edge using cold-water-soluble stabilizer, trace the design on the fabric, baste fabric and stabilizer together, and stitch along the design outline. Cut away only fabric inside the open areas of the design (above). Place fabric and stabilizer in an inverted hoop with the stabilizer against the machine bed; embroider the design, covering all raw edges with stitches (above, right). When embroidery is complete, trim away large areas of unused stabilizer; dissolve the rest under running water (right). Lay flat to dry.

can readily work with; mine is 8 in. If my design is large, I break it into several sections, each of which will fit my hoop, and then join the pieces by stitching between them after most of the embroidery is done.

Your basic materials will also include scissors and thread. Any scissors will do, but I really like tiny, curved manicure scissors, as they reach where bulky scissors can't. All machine sewing threads are appropriate for dissolving fabrics, but threads with a sheen work especially well. Rayon threads come in delicious colors and are available under the names of Madeira, Natesh, and Sulky, among others. Variegated threads give interesting results, as do many metallic threads. Try using a contrasting color in the bobbin, or threading two different colors through the needle together.

Stretch the soluble fabric tightly in the hoop, then pull and adjust to eliminate any loose areas. Invert the hoop so the inner ring is visible when you are working. Gently ease the outer hoop up a bit to allow the stretched fabric to lie flush against the bed

of the sewing machine so that the stitches will form correctly.

The simplest straight-stitch machine will make wonderful embroideries, as long as it is in good working condition. Complicated, computerized machines will also do well but certainly aren't necessary. To prepare your machine for free embroidery, lower the feed dog or cover the teeth with a metal plate, as specified for your machine. Then set the stitch length at 0, remove the presser foot, and replace it with a darning foot (see *Threads* No. 36, p. 16). You can sew without a foot, but remember to lower the presser bar to engage the machine's tension.

Wind several bobbins before you start (stopping later to wind bobbins breaks the rhythm of your work), then thread your machine and adjust the tension to balance the needle and bobbin threads. Always pull the bobbin thread through to the right side of your material before you begin. After sewing a few stitches, you can trim both thread ends close to the fabric and stitch back over them to lock them in.   ⇨

Stitching hints

Test the technique by stitching your name on the soluble fabric in your hoop several times, just to develop a feeling for the rhythm of movement. Look at what you have sewn and visualize which letters would hold together if the background were dissolved. Unless adjacent letters are tied together by stitching back and forth between them, they will not hold their shape once the stabilizer is gone. Practice gauging your speed as well as the direction in which you manipulate the hoop. Learn to control your embroidery rather than letting it control you.

After mastering your name, draw the outline of a simple shape on the soluble fabric. Use a lead pencil, or a marker that won't bleed into the embroidery during the dissolving process. Stitch completely around the outline, then consider the central areas. Do you want them to be solid, or open for a mesh effect? If you want the area solid you have two choices: You can sew a grid, or you can move the hoop in a circular or random pattern, making certain that you stitch back into the previously stitched areas occasionally, as shown in the drawings below. For lacy designs, try stitching a grid or lattice, then filling some areas but not others, or making open, circular stitches as shown. Always ask yourself if those lines of stitching will stay in place when the background has disappeared. If you are stitching one area next to another, be certain the threads overlap occasionally to hold the areas together. It's often a good idea to return to the original outline and sew over it one more time. Finally, hold the piece to the light and examine it carefully. Are all the areas connected? Are there threads that aren't connected to their neighbors? If there are, add stitching to connect them.

The dissolving process

Dissolve your first experiment to see how you have done. Remove the hoop, then trim away large areas of unsewn fabric. If you are using hot-water-soluble fabric, drop the embroidery into a pan of simmering water. This is frightening, as the piece will appear to curl and shrink. It may be necessary to swish it around a bit to remove all the PVA fibers, but in a few minutes there will be nothing left but the embroidery. The photo below shows an embroidery after the stabilizer has been removed. The embroidery will have shrunk somewhat, but it can be carefully stretched into its original shape and size. Pin it to a padded surface to dry for several hours, or use a hair dryer for faster results.

The cold-water fabric dissolves the same way, except that the water temperature is unimportant. This allows you more options: pin it to a padded surface and then spray the fabric until it has dissolved, hold it under running tap water as shown on p. 19, steam it, or immerse it in a pan of water. Allow at least 45 seconds for the fabric to dissolve in water, longer with spraying or steaming.

The manufacturer of water-soluble fabrics states that both forms are nontoxic. However, as with any craft supply, it's always a good idea to clean up thoroughly after use, or reserve special pans which are not used in food preparation.

Think of more uses for this material and technique: Sandwiching bits of threads, fabric scraps, ribbons, and other items between layers of dissolving fabric holds them in place while you stitch over them. For more texture, add beads or sequins (make sure that they are colorfast), or use a heavier thread in the bobbin to give the piece a couched look. Make some jewelry to match your just-constructed dress, collars with fabric pieces and lacy areas combined, embellishments for anything, decorative boxes and baskets. Create your own magic, large or small. □

Cindy Hickok's work has appeared in international exhibitions. She currently teaches workshops on using soluble fabrics. For information, write to WSF Workshops, 523 Briar Path, Houston, TX 77079.

Following their guide, machine-embroidered tourists wend their way through one of the author's free-standing miniatures. All the figures, each about 1½ in. tall, were stitched on organza-like Solvron stabilizer. A hot water bath dissolved the stabilizer, leaving only the threads.

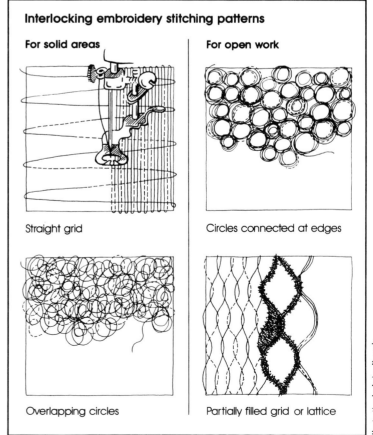

Interlocking embroidery stitching patterns

For solid areas

Straight grid

Overlapping circles

For open work

Circles connected at edges

Partially filled grid or lattice

Illustration by Laine Roundy

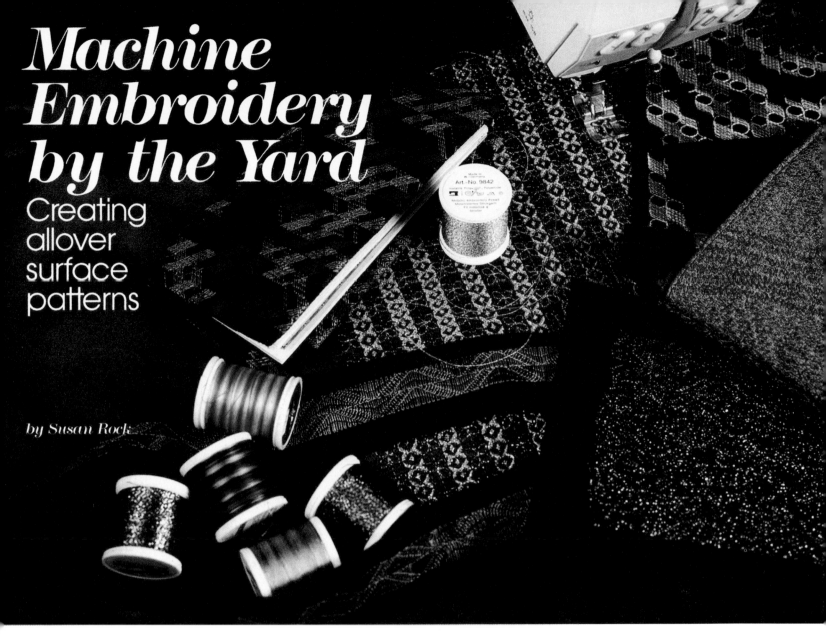

Machine Embroidery by the Yard

Creating allover surface patterns

by Susan Rock

hen I proved to myself that I could create new and unique fabrics with the decorative stitches in my new computerized sewing machine, I realized that I had finally answered that age-old question: "What *are* these pattern stitches good for, anyway?"

The trick is to find stitches and combinations of stitches that are effective when stitched side by side all over the surface of the fabric. It helps to have lots of patterns to choose from, and as wide a stitch as possible, but even plain old 4mm zigzag can make lovely surfaces, as we'll see below, so you don't have to have a fancy computerized machine. The fabrics I've made this way are thick, and fairly stiff, like lightweight upholstery fabrics, so they're perfect for book covers, tote bags, purses, belts, and straps, like those in the photo above; and even for small insets on wearables.

I made my discovery almost by accident.

Determined to find a use for my wealth of decorative stitches, I started by stitching a sample of all the preset patterns. Many appeared useless, but some were elegant and intriguing. I didn't want to bother with an embroidery hoop, so I was stitching on a medium-weight fabric on top of a non-fusible tear-away stabilizer.

Somewhat at random, I chose for my first experiment a firm, black cotton/poly fabric (all-cotton is usually too soft), and a vivid red, blue, green, and yellow variegated two-ply, 40-weight rayon thread, with plain black machine embroidery cotton in the bobbin (see *Threads* No. 34, p. 20, for more on sewing thread). My first step was to stitch a straight vertical row of a loose, open stitch pattern. Next I chose a densely embroidered program and stitched it right next to the first pattern. The two rows looked good together, so I added a third row which was a repeat of the first row, and I continued interchanging rows until the black fabric was covered with

machine embroidery. As I watched the design develop, I was ecstatic: I was creating my own patterned fabric! I've been exploring the possibilites ever since.

Setting up

Stitching in an embroidery hoop would be a real pain for patterns that cover the entire fabric, so I still always stitch on a medium-weight fabric that's been underlaid with a piece of non-fusible tear-away stabilizer (available at most notions counters, or by mail from Treadleart, 25834 Narbonne Ave., Lomita, CA 90717; 213-534-8372) to prevent puckering and distortion of the fabric. I always start with a new

Susan Rock uses the programmed stitches in a computerized sewing machine to create allover surface designs on yardage. The resulting fabrics are light upholstery-weight, appropriate for purses, bags, book covers, and some clothing embellishment.

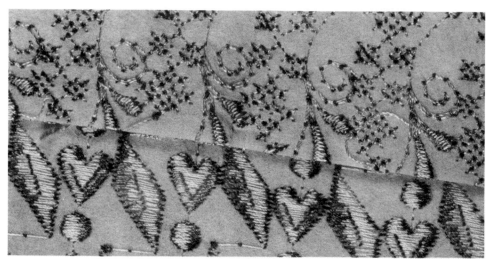

Rock loosens the top thread tension, so the top threads are pulled to the underside as shown above and can't be seen. As a result, no matter what top thread she's using, she can use white or black thread in the bobbin. All the designs below are variations of the dense row/loose row side-by-side repeat that Rock found the most effective for allover stripe designs. Variegated thread looks best, except that metallic threads seem to work equally well whether variegated or not.

90/14 universal needle. This is also a good needle choice for construction sewing with these embroidered fabrics.

I loosen the top tension a little to ensure that the top thread pulls to the back of the fabric and that the bobbin thread is never visible, at least when I'm stitching satin-stitch-based stitches. This way I can use the same bobbin thread (two-ply 50-weight machine embroidery cotton) no matter what top threads I choose. I usually choose white bobbin thread, unless I'm stitching on black fabric, in which case I'll use black thread so the open-stitch patterns don't show little dots of white. Looser top tension also helps prevent puckering; bobbin tension remains normal. I adjust down two numbers on my machine; try different settings on your machine to find the right balance between concealing the bobbin thread and putting too much top thread on the bottom layer. You can see the back of my fabrics at top left.

Choosing threads and stitches

As I continued experimenting, I examined my sample swatch for other open stitch patterns to combine with dense stitch patterns. Many patterns I had thought useless now seemed very interesting. As before I stitched them side by side and close together, so there were no spacing problems to worry about. Almost all the dense/open pattern pairs I selected were successful, and the designs I like best still tend to be combinations of loose, even-textured stitches with more figurative, satinstitch-based patterns, like the ones at left. The possible combinations are almost endless. Single patterns repeated over and over also work best for me if they're loose and open, like the ones on the facing page, but try all of the designs on your machine to see what they do when massed together. Experiment with the stitch length controls to see if you can open up dense patterns to create interesting textures.

I still find variegated threads to be far more exciting than solid colors, because they automatically produce color patterns that work across the surface of your design, creating counter-rhythms that add immeasurably to the visual interest. Metallic threads, either solid or variegated, also work very well, perhaps because the play of reflected light creates movement and dimension in much the same way as changing colors. Of course, for more restrained effects, solid colors can be beautiful, too.

Naturally, the choice of base fabric will be important to the finished design. When you use a fabric that matches your thread you'll end up with an embossed look. If you select a fabric that matches one color in a variegated thread you will end up "losing" stitches against the background. This is not an undesirable effect. For the fabric I made into the checkbook cover shown on p. 21, I used black twill and stabilizer, and a gold, red, and black 40-weight rayon thread. The black thread disappeared on the black fabric, producing a random pattern of red and gold. I enjoy seeing the segments of red and gold and then apparently no stitching.

Zigzag patterns

For those who don't have an embroidery programmed machine, good old zigzag can be worked into wonderful tweedy, plaidlike patterns when you use multi-colored rayon thread. In the examples shown at right, I set my zigzag stitches to 4mm wide and 1mm long. I first covered the fabric with abutting vertical rows of zigzag. At the end of each row I left the needle down in the right-hand position and simply turned the fabric 180° Next I repeated the zigzag, horizontally covering the fabric, then stitched in two more directions, diagonally right to left and then left to right.

If you do the diagonal stitching first, followed by vertical and horizontal layers, you'll get a more on-grain, mottled effect.

To create the muted, heathery fabric I used for the zippered bag on p. 21, I used three solid-color threads: a turquoise, a purple, and a medium blue, stitched horizontally, vertically, then once diagonally on medium blue fabric, with a few rows of bright pink stitched in the remaining diagonal direction for emphasis. ☐

Susan Rock is Technical Sewing Director for Madeira Marketing, Ltd. She recently taped a machine embroidery segment for the PBS series Crafting in the '90s.

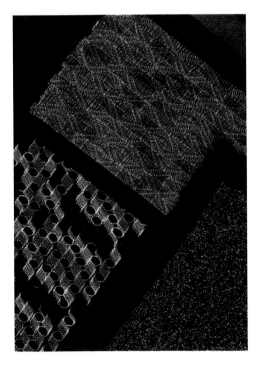

If you choose to repeat a single pattern all over, try loose, open stitches like those at left for best results. Ordinary zigzag stitches (above) at maximum width combine to create varied surfaces when stitched vertically, then horizontally, then diagonally across plain fabric. If you stitch the diagonal rows first, the final effect is more on grain, less diagonal.

Secrets of Professional Machine Appliqué

Careful planning and a toolbox of edge finishes make the difference

by Diane Hendry

i spend my days designing and constructing detailed machine-appliquéd garments for a New York fashion designer. But occasionally I find time for a personal project, like the vest shown on the facing page, that allows me to have fun with the techniques I work with every day: machine appliqué of decorative fabrics using zigzag and straight stitches and a regular presser foot, plus a little hand sewing, when it makes sense.

Using the vest as a specific example, I'll go over the techniques in detail, covering both the materials I chose and the processes I employed. These techniques are appropriate whenever you want to create a decorative effect or image on fabric, and they can be used even when you want to retain some drape and softness (I've even used them for curtains and upholstery fabrics).

Basic equipment required

Even though I work with an industrial sewing machine at home, I don't do anything with it that I couldn't do on a domestic one. For easy manipulation of the fabric layers as you stitch around complex shapes, you'll want the machine bed to be level with your table, and the bigger the table, the better. The only material I'll be describing that's probably not already in your sewing room is spray adhesive, and you can get that anywhere art supplies are sold.

My materials typically include glitzy yarns, narrow ribbons, felt, and leather, along with assorted sheers, nets, and lots of textured opaque fabrics, plus many colors of thread. A great variety of options in your raw materials certainly makes for a varied and interesting piece, but just as important is varying the stitching and edge-finishing techniques you use on each element. If I'd used a plain satin stitch on every edge in my vest, even these wonderful fabrics would have had less impact and less magic.

An overview of the process

Whether it's a collection of fabrics that inspires a particular image or an image that suggests the kind of fabrics I want to use, I always start my appliquéd garment projects with a full-scale drawing of the design, worked out precisely on the shapes of the pattern I've chosen. You can lay out a completed drawing over tracings of the

If I'd used a plain satin stitch on every edge, even these wonderful fabrics would have had less impact.

pattern pieces you're using. You can also make separate drawings of the elements and designs you want to use, cut them out, and experiment with different placements of them on your pattern.

My next step is usually to select the background fabric and stabilize it with a soft fusible if it seems flimsy; I wind up fusing most light- to medium-weight fabrics, as I did with the iridescent purple silk in my vest. Even a thin interfacing eliminates the need for an embroidery hoop. I then cut the pattern with generous ¾-in. seam allowances, because everything shifts, pulls, and distorts a little as each successive layer is stitched down. When your background is cut out you can trace position lines for major pieces from your drawing onto the fused pieces (I use a wheel and dressmakers' tracing paper), and start working out the order in which you'll want to attach your layers. I trim the seam allowances of each pattern piece to the exact pattern shape after all the appliqué is completed by laying the pattern over the stitched fabric layers, shifting the pattern if necessary to accommodate any changes that have occurred.

At this stage, I usually make up the individual elements that will become appliqués. Naturally, I continually experiment and re-evaluate how the parts are working together as each one is finished. When all the parts are eventually in place and stitched down, I lay the original pattern pieces on top to check that no details will be lost in seams and that the design matches up where necessary across seamlines. Finally, I trim the seam allowances and join the pieces, then add the lining if the project is a garment. Let's go over the processes I used to make and attach the individual elements, then look quickly at how this particular project came together. ⇨

Match the edge finish to the fabric you're stitching: straight stitch for nonraveling felt and leather, ribbon-covered zigzag for chiffons, and hand stitches for silk bouclé.

From *Threads* magazine (June 1994) 53:70-73

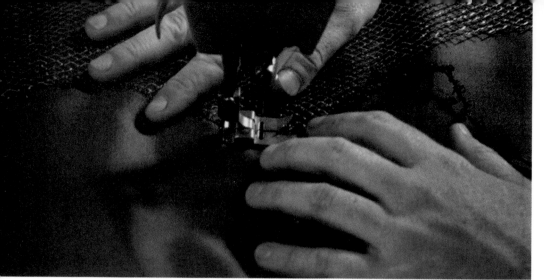

Fabric edges gain definition if yarn or narrow ribbon is machine stitched over them. Zigzag over yarns and straight-stitch over ribbons, gripping the fabric lightly with both hands for maximum control and quick changes in direction.

Nonraveling materials simplify stitch-downs, are easy to cut into complex shapes, and add textural variety. On the sand at bottom, from left: a speckled suede starfish, blue felt seaweed, and a crab from hand-painted felt. Anemone stalks at center were faced and edgestitched.

Stitching ravelly fabrics

The most basic technique I use is just to stitch down the edges of simple layers to the background with either a straight or a zigzag stitch. Anything that ravels, I stitch with a zigzag; anything that doesn't, I stitch with a straight stitch.

Adding decorative trim—I usually finish wovens by stitching a decorative ribbon or yarn on top of the first stitching, as I'm doing in the photo at left, after trimming any stray threads or missed edges. Defining the edges in this way adds greatly to the clarity and polish of the finished piece. As you can see, I use an ordinary presser foot, pivoting the fabric while stitching to control the process; the photo shows the hand position I find most useful. I zigzag over yarn, but usually straight-stitch over ribbons.

Applying spray adhesive—For temporarily holding down complex shapes in a wide variety of fabrics as you stitch them, nothing beats spray adhesive. Lay the fabric to be sprayed right side down on scrap paper, and give it a delicate spray that will hold lightly when the shape is pressed in place.

Here's an example of the benefits of spray adhesive when working with light, transparent fabrics like chiffon: To make the long, wavy fronds of two-tone seaweed shown in the photo at lower left and on p. 25, I first cut the darker fabric to the final shape by laying it over the original drawing. Because it's chiffon, I can see through it, so I can cut it out without the need for a separate pattern piece. Then I sprayed the back of an untrimmed chunk of the pale green and pressed it over the first piece. I was able to stitch the two together down the middle responding just to the sinuous shape I wanted without worrying about catching the edge at the same time. After sewing, I lifted the pale green and trimmed it to the stitching on one side, and to the shape of the piece underneath on the other. Then I sprayed the whole thing and pressed it where I wanted it on the background, to be stitched and covered with thin ribbon.

Appliquéing nonraveling fabrics

Since these edges need only a straight stitch, they're among my favorites. Real and fake leathers and suedes of every description, felts, nets, lace, and mesh all fall into this category, so the most dramatic elements are often the easiest to stitch.

Felt—Felt is easy to find and wonderfully versatile, because you can cut it into very precise shapes. The sea shell, crab, and turquoise star-shaped seaweed shown at the bottom of the facing page were made this way. I cut the crab from white felt and painted it with thin acrylic paints before stitching. To create small spots of color I used felt in two ways. For the red ovals against the blue background of the coral on the vest front (p. 25), I cut little bits of felt and handstitched them, but for the yellow spots on green just below the coral, I first covered yellow felt with green chiffon and zigzagged little circles, then cut away the green to reveal the yellow underneath.

Leather—Leathery textures can add variety to almost any piece, and you can get a lot of mileage out of a little chunk. Both the starfish and the seahorse are leather. In both cases I traced the original drawing in reverse, then sprayed the back of the tracing and stuck it onto the back of the leather so it would be easy to cut the shapes precisely. You can use an X-Acto knife and/or scissors, whichever works best on your material. For contrast, I also stuck a glitzy fabric to the back of each cut-out leather shape and stitched that from the front before trimming the excess and stitching down the finished piece. Test all leathers to see if you can touch them with an iron; most don't mind, but a few can't take any heat or steam, so check first.

Zigzag stitches—Occasionally, a nonwoven needs a zigzag instead of a straight stitch. The wonderful brain-coral-shaped lines of the background net simply called for a loose zigzag that followed the lines as invisibly as possible; a straight stitch would have looked awful.

Faced shapes and stitched textures

To create a raised edge and/or a clean finish with a woven, you can face the shape and turn it right sides out, then tack it down by hand or machine. The photos below show an easy way to face all sides of even very complex shapes. Once the shape is faced, you can slip-stitch through the underlayer to preserve the raised edge, as I did for the blue/purple coral in the photos below, or machine stitch it flat, as on the reddish anemone stalks on the facing page.

The blue and gold coral stalks opposite the seahorse on the vest front are hybrids—part faced, part turned-under edge, and are also the result of a texturing technique you can see on the gold-toned stalks. I faced the blue ovals at the top of each stalk and machine stitched them down. But for the stalks, I wanted a different texture. First I cut a blue base layer for each stalk. Then I laid a large bias piece of gold chiffon over the blue and stitched down the folds you can see on the vest front with contrast thread one at a time in a spreading pattern, starting in the middle and working out to each side. At the edges, I trimmed the remaining chiffon to extend a bit beyond the base fabric and folded it under, then straight-stitched the whole thing to the background, blending into the stitching that holds down the folds in the middle.

Assembly

Anything stitched under something else has to be stitched down first. In my piece, the main dividing line between foreground and background was the top edge of the raw silk bouclé I used for the sandy ocean floor. Everything behind that had to be completed first. For the background, I assembled the various layers by first spraying and tacking them down to confirm their positions, then stitched, lifting edges when necessary to stitch bottom layers. Next I checked the sand line by laying the drawing over the work. Then I pressed under the bouclé and handstitched it.

At this point I paused to make the appliqués as described and stitched them over the sand and background layers (except for the seahorse and larger beads, which couldn't take heat or steam). To reduce bulk under the large, stiff crab, I trimmed the bouclé underneath.

After a good allover press, I added the missing pieces, then attached the lining by machine. To keep the lining from peeking out anywhere, I hand tacked the entire perimeter about ¼ in. inside the seamline on the lining side, without stitching through to the front. The finishing touch was to hand sew on graduated opalescent beads to create the illusion of bubbles floating to the surface. □

Diane Hendry is assistant to the designer at Koos for De Wilde Ltd., in New York City (see Threads *No. 26, pp. 28-33). She freelances in interiors, signage, and commercial pattern design.*

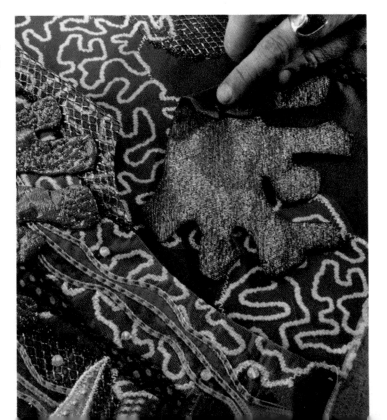

Facing a complex shape: (Top left) Layer a heavy paper pattern without seam allowances over chiffon and fabric (right side up), pin layers together, and stitch completely around pattern.

(Bottom left) Cut out, leaving ⅛-in. seam allowance. Clip into curves, and snip an opening in the chiffon.

(Right) Turn shape right side out, press, and handstitch to the garment.

by Carol Neumann

*t*he heirloom garment, once an exclusively Southern style, is enjoying a revival. Home sewers in every state are lavishing their time and skill on white-on-white christening gowns, starched and ruffly children's dress-up and party clothes, nostalgic wedding dresses, blouses, and lingerie, as well as pillows and trappings for boudoir, ring bearers, and nurseries. The common elements are fine, translucent fabrics; lots of trims and lace; and the nearly invisible seams needed to hold them all together as exquisitely as possible.

The current revival is aided by the happy fact that the zigzag sewing machine (and sometimes even the serger) can mimic, with amazing speed and quality, many of the hallmark techniques of the handsewn masterpieces of the past. These hand techniques were themselves revived in the 1960s as French handsewing (so called because nuns in pre-Revolutionary France had probably invented them) with the work of Southern masters like Sarah Howard Stone and Margaret Pierce, whose books were the first written accounts of the subject since the craft had been developed. The machine-sewn adaptations are still widely known as French handsewing by machine, or more simply, as heirloom sewing.

I was fascinated by the tiny seams and invisible stitches of French handsewing and by the idea that I could come close on my sewing machine. I wanted to make a project, preferably a garment, but my personal fashion style leans more to Armani suits (if I could afford them!) than to pastel, ruffled dresses. So I resolved to make myself a garment (photo at left) that would express my personality yet allow me to use heirloom-sewing techniques.

Basic skills and materials

The technique at the heart of French handsewing is rolling and whipping, a method for finishing raw fabric edges as narrowly and delicately as possible. Before being attached to any kind of lace or trim, every fabric edge is tightly rolled 1½ times (around the needle to start, then just around itself) and covered with ⅛-in.-long whipstitches that wrap around the roll like candy-cane stripes. When done correctly, the stitches show only the wrong side, but this takes skill, practice, and above all, time.

Machine methods duplicate this effect by zigzagging (or serging) right over raw edges in such a way that the edge curls up

Heirloom Sewing

Sewing machines and sergers make it easy to duplicate the handsewn glories of the past

Carol Neumann's wool-challis blouse, based on Burda pattern 5860, simulates handsewn techniques but is entirely machine-made.

From *Threads* magazine (February 1990) 27:46-49

inside the stitches as they form. It's neither as soft nor as invisible as the hand method, but it comes close to it and takes very little time. The best part is that it can be done at the same time the edge is joined to the attached trim, as described below.

Trims include French and English laces, beading, eyelet, and *entredeux,* sometimes called veining, all shown in the photo at right. They're available in white, off-white, and ecru. Embroidered trims may involve several pastel threads on a white or ecru background. Laces and eyelets may be insertions, which have two straight edges; edgings, which have one scalloped edge; or beadings, which have larger holes for the threading of ribbon. Look for 100% cotton or blends of 90% cotton and 10% nylon. Polyester trims and laces don't work well; they feel scratchy and resist shaping when you're trying to curve motifs.

Entredeux is the most common trim in heirloom sewing; it resembles hemstitching and has batiste seam allowances on both sides. It's available in narrow to wide widths; the wider widths can also be used for beading. *Entredeux* adds decorative strength to seams and should be used whenever fabric is joined to other trims. It can also be used when fabric is joined to fabric; otherwise, the norm is ⅛-in.-wide French seams. Look for smooth, flat *entredeux* with holes that are evenly sized and completely open. The right side is raised and is a little shinier than the wrong side.

The best fabrics for heirloom sewing are high-thread-count plain weaves of cotton, wool, linen, and some cotton/polyester blends. Since synthetic fibers tend to be wiry and resist rolling, handsewers avoid them, but imperial batiste, made of cotton/polyester, is an alternative if you can't stand wrinkles, and you'll be using machine techniques. The most popular fabrics for today's uses are 100% cotton Swiss batistes, which have a delicate sheen. They wrinkle incredibly, which just adds to the authenticity of your heirloom. Fine wool challis and handkerchief linen are other suitable alternatives. All of these fabrics are available in several pastel shades, as well as white, off-white, and ecru. Interfacing is usually not used in heirloom sewing, since it would show through the sheer fabrics.

As for all good sewing, the fabric must be on grain. This is especially true for fabric strips that are assembled together with trims into new fabrics for details like collars and yokes. Begin by clipping the selvage and pulling a crosswise thread. Trim the fabric on the pulled thread; then pull another crosswise thread at the desired width, and cut as before. Using strips cut on the crosswise grain is an efficient way to use these expensive fabrics. Large garment pieces,

The basic trims in heirloom sewing, from top to bottom: entredeux, used in seams; beading, through which ribbon can be threaded; lace edging (one French and one English); and a combined trim of entredeux and embroidery.

like those for skirts, are, of course, cut on the lengthwise grain. You'll find it helpful for machine techniques to spray-starch and press all trims and fabrics before sewing.

Extra-fine white thread may be used on all these colors and fabrics; it blends into pastels invisibly. Cotton machine-embroidery thread is a good choice that won't add bulk to the seams. With such fine thread, use a size 8 (60) or 9 (75) needle. Check for burrs on the needle point frequently, and change the needle after every five hours of sewing, even if it feels smooth.

Closures should be selected carefully so as not to damage the garment. Tiny, handmade buttonholes and pearl buttons work well. Another option is to use beauty pins. Beauty pins are small bar pins that efficiently close the garment and add to its elegance. The pins may be gold-plated, to which a monogram is sometimes added, or handpainted with tiny flowers or to match the color of the garment.

Designing a project

Any pattern that is loose-fitting and calls for soft, fine fabrics may be adapted to French handsewing. A ¼-in. seam allowance is always used with hand or machine techniques, so adjust seam allowances on

patterns that have ⅝-in. allowances. Many patterns are specifically designed for French handsewing (see supplies, p. 31), but there's a lot of fun and creativity involved in designing your own project. The drawback in creating your own design is the measuring and calculating necessary to determine exactly how much of all the trims you'll need.

The simplest place to incorporate heirloom embellishing techniques is in the details, like yokes, cuffs, and collars. Start designing with the widest or most prominent trim at the center, and work away from the center symmetrically. Plan for flat fabric at curved areas (armholes) to make it easier to join parts of the garment. Another appropriate place is around the lower edge of a skirt. This is called a "fancy band" and may be as narrow or wide as you like. Sleeves are perfect for embellishments, beading and ribbon can replace elastic, and edging can finish the hem. If you're really ambitious and cost is not a factor, you could make entire sections or the whole garment of pieced-together trims and lace.

If your plan calls for lace insertion, edgings, and *entredeux* in a few seams, you can cut out the pattern pieces in fabric and insert laces and *entredeux* as you come to them. If a section involves many rows of lace, pin tucks, embroidery, etc., it's best to create the fabric for that piece and then cut out the pattern shape from it.

To create fabric for a pattern piece, first trace a full-size pattern (right and left sides) on a large piece of paper. Draw a square or rectangle around the pattern that's about 1 in. larger than the piece. Looking at the trims you want to use, sketch a design to fit the rectangle. Then sew pin tucks and work embroidery on strips of fabric in widths to match your design. Cut all strips and trims to the size of the rectangle or square, sew the strips together, and press to block the fabric. Center the pattern on the heirloom fabric and cut out the garment shape. Yokes and collars may be one layer of the heirloom fabric, or they can be lined with the garment fabric.

For my project, I chose Burda pattern 5860. It has a stand-up collar, which enables me to wear a favorite brooch, and which would be appropriate to wear with a suit or a silk or velvet skirt. I found a wool-challis fabric suitable for cooler climates. Buttons and buttonholes would interrupt the design I created for the center-front panels, so instead I chose hand-painted beauty pins to close the blouse. I embroidered small X's at the center fronts to help me position the pins.

The collar and cuffs are made from fabric I designed, using wide, pointed lace edging and insertion lace. Both are joined to the garment with *entredeux.* The cuffs are closed with thread loops and small buttons, as beauty pins would be difficult to fasten. The collar and cuffs are loose-fitting for comfort. This allows the lace collar points to curl outward naturally from the neck.

I joined the sleeve/yoke to the body of the blouse with *entredeux*. The *entredeux* strengthens the seam and emphasizes the design. Curved lace insertion in the back of the blouse adds elegance and repeats the curve of the sleeve/yoke seam. The length of the sleeve would have been a good place for more embellishment. However, I like to wear shoulder pads, and I didn't want trims that would expose a shoulder pad, so I left the sleeves plain.

Heirloom-sewing techniques

The first thing to establish is the zigzag-stitch length, which will remain the same for the entire project. The zigzag-stitch length is determined by the distance between the holes of the *entredeux*. Cut a 3-in. to 4-in. strip of your *entredeux;* then set the machine for a zigzag stitch that's 3 mm wide (⅛ in.) and about 12 to 16 stitches per inch. Position the *entredeux* so the needle swings from a hole of the *entredeux* to the batiste seam allowance. Adjust the stitch length so the needle stitches once into each hole of the *entredeux*. Write down the stitch-length setting so you can quickly adjust your machine each time you use the zigzag stitch. If you use several sizes of *entredeux* in a project, you'll need to adjust the stitch length for each size.

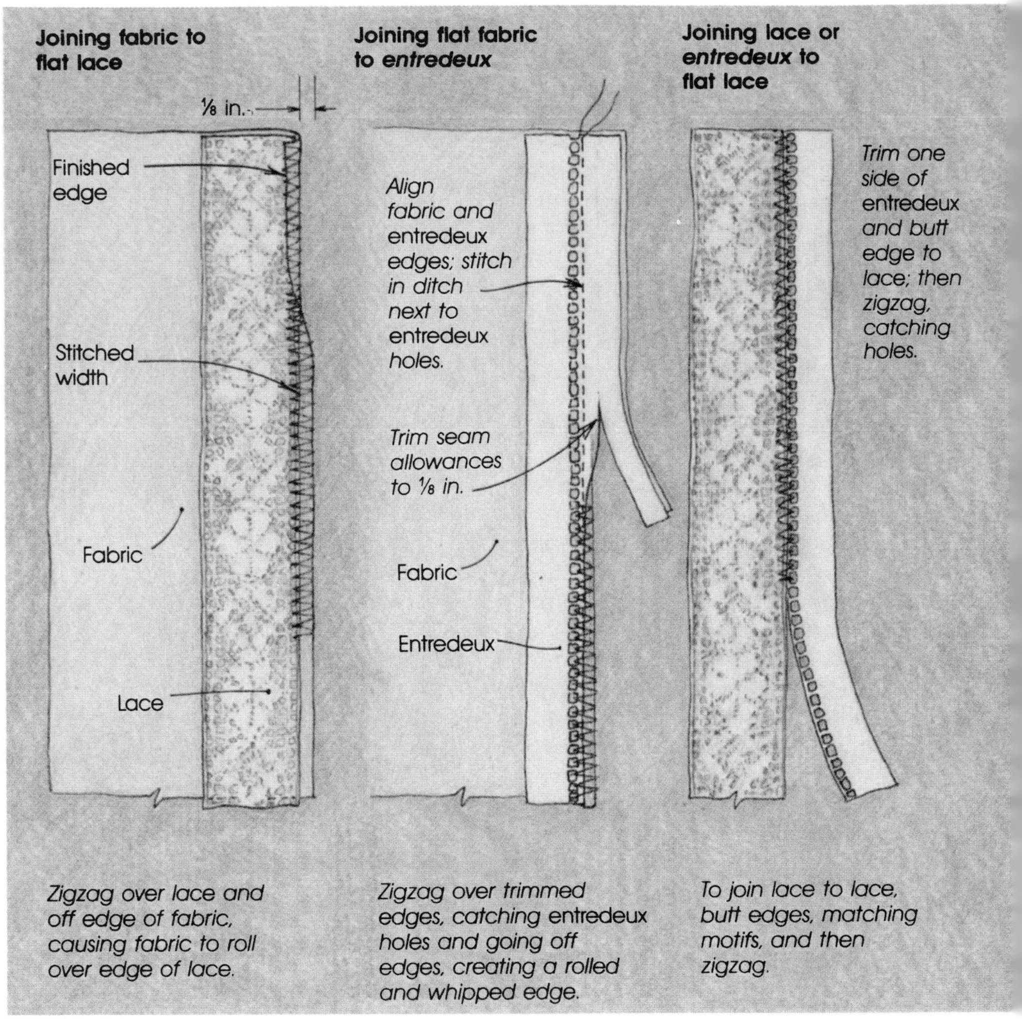

Joining fabric to flat lace—On a conventional zigzag machine place starched and pressed strips right sides together with the fabric on the bottom and extending about ⅛ in. beyond the lace at the right edge. Set the zigzag-stitch width so the left "zig" is ⅛ in. onto the top strip and the right "zag" extends just off the edge of the bottom strip, as in the first drawing at right, above. As the needle moves back and forth, the bottom strip rolls over the lace. You may need to loosen the upper-thread tension and adjust the stitch width to get good results. On the serger, adjust for a rolled-hem setting with the stitch length at 2 mm to 3 mm. Place fabric and flat lace right sides together, edges even, and stitch so the needle is about ⅛ in. onto the lace. Press the rolled seam toward the fabric.

Joining flat fabric to *entredeux*—On the sewing machine, place starched and pressed strips right sides together, edges even, *entredeux* on top, and stitch in the ditch next to the holes of the *entredeux*. Trim the seam allowances to a scant ⅛ in. (center drawing at right, above). Complete the seam by zigzagging as above. On the serger,

Joining fabric to flat lace

⅛ in.

Finished edge

Stitched width

Fabric

Lace

Zigzag over lace and off edge of fabric, causing fabric to roll over edge of lace.

Joining flat fabric to *entredeux*

Align fabric and entredeux edges; stitch in ditch next to entredeux holes.

Trim seam allowances to ⅛ in.

Fabric

Entredeux

Zigzag over trimmed edges, catching entredeux holes and going off edges, creating a rolled and whipped edge.

Joining lace or *entredeux* to flat lace

Trim one side of entredeux and butt edge to lace; then zigzag, catching holes.

To join lace to lace, butt edges, matching motifs, and then zigzag.

Illustrations by Christopher Clapp

mark a line on the serger presser foot from the needle to the end of the foot. Use the line as a guide to stitch in the ditch next to the holes of the *entredeux*, using a rolled-hem setting. In either case, press the rolled seam toward the fabric.

Joining flat lace to lace or *entredeux*—For *entredeux*, trim one seam allowance off completely, and butt the trimmed edge to the lace, right sides up. For laces, butt edges, right sides up. Be sure to match the motifs in the lace strips. Stitch lace or *entredeux*, using the zigzag stitch (width and length determined above) to cover the join (drawing at right, above).

Lace insertion—Lace insertion is very elegant. It looks difficult to do, but it's not, and it takes very little time. You can cut the pattern piece from the fabric before applying the lace so you'll have manageable sizes of fabric to work with. You can insert the lace in the fabric in a straight row or as a diamond, loop, oval, teardrop, bow, or any other shape. Trace the center of the design onto the fabric, using a marking pen with disappearing ink. Center the starched and

pressed lace over the line, and pin it to the fabric. To shape curves, position the lace over the design line and pin it on the outer curve only. Use a needle to pick up a heavy thread at the lace edge (called the heading) along the inside curve (drawing at left, facing page). Pull the thread and adjust the fullness until the lace lies completely flat; then steam-press it to shrink out the excess fullness, and pin the inside edge.

Set the stitch length as you would for *entredeux*, and set the width just wide enough to cover the heading. Zigzag both edges of the lace to the fabric. Then cut the fabric under the lace on the marked line, and press the fabric toward the stitching. From the right side, zigzag-stitch each lace edge over the first stitching again, catching the folded fabric underneath. The final step is to trim the excess fabric on the wrong side, close to the stitching. I recommend that you use a duck-bill scissors to trim close so that you don't cut the stitches.

At corners, turn under the excess lace to create a mitered, or diagonal, seam and finger-press the fold. Try to miter corners between the lace motifs, or match the motifs at the fold. A continuous strip of lace makes

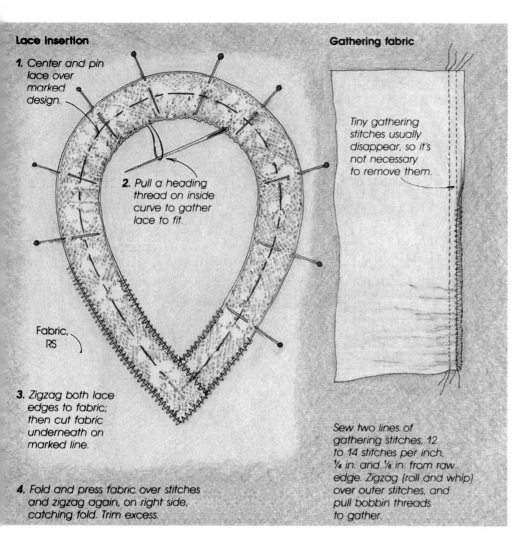

Lace insertion

1. Center and pin lace over marked design.

2. Pull a heading thread on inside curve to gather lace to fit.

Fabric, RS

3. Zigzag both lace edges to fabric; then cut fabric underneath on marked line.

4. Fold and press fabric over stitches and zigzag again, on right side, catching fold. Trim excess.

Gathering fabric

Tiny gathering stitches usually disappear, so it's not necessary to remove them.

Sew two lines of gathering stitches, 12 to 14 stitches per inch, ¼ in. and ⅛ in. from raw edge. Zigzag (roll and whip) over outer stitches, and pull bobbin threads to gather.

Further reading

McMakin, Kathy B. *French Sewing by Serger*, 1988. Self-published: Albright Partners, 1205 E. Cleermont Circle, Huntsville, AL 35801.

Pullen, Martha. *French Hand Sewing by Machine I*, 1983; *French Hand Sewing by Machine II*, 1985. Self-published: 518 Madison St., Huntsville, AL 35801; (800) 547-4176. *Sells supplies; catalog, $1.*

Stone, Melissa. *French Hand Sewing for Machine*, 1987. Self-published: Sarah Howard Stone, 514 Cloverdale Rd., Montgomery, AL 36106; (205) 262-7154. *Sells supplies; catalog, $2.*

Turner, Mildred. *Mimi's Machine Heirloom Sewing*, 1987. Self-published: Mimi's Smock Shoppe, 502 Balsam Rd., Hazelwood, NC 28738; (704) 452-3455. *Sells supplies.*

Patterns, fabric, and books

Garden Fairies Trading Company
Box 5770
Santa Rosa, CA 95402
(707) 526-5907
Catalog, $3.50; catalog and swatches, $6.

Hummingbird House
Box 4242, Dept. T
Palm Desert, CA 92261-4242
(716) 754-8833
Catalog, $3.

The Smocking Bonnet
Box 555, Dept TH
Cooksville, MD 21723
(800) 524-1678
Catalog, $5.

Beauty pins

Dancing Needles
102 Kennett Rd.
Old Hickory, TN 37138
(615) 847-8675; *catalog, $1.*

matching difficult, so you may want to cut individual lengths. Remove the lace from the fabric, and with a short, narrow zigzag, stitch the corner(s) on the fold line, from the wrong side. Trim the excess lace close to the stitching. Spray-starch and press the lace; pin in place again and stitch and trim as above.

At overlaps, decide beforehand which layer will stay, and position that layer on top. Then zigzag, following its edges, and trim away the underlayer later.

Pin tucks—Pin tucks require a twin needle and a pin-tuck presser foot, but with these tools they're easy embellishments for heirloom sewing. Remember to allow extra fabric for the width of each tuck (⅛ in. per tuck for a 2.0 twin needle). Plan for an uneven number of tucks, with the middle tuck at the center of the fabric strip.

Begin by spray-starching and pressing an on-grain fabric strip. Set the stitch length at 12 to 14 stitches per inch, and tighten the upper-thread tension slightly. Pull a thread the length of the strip to mark the center tuck and to ensure that the tucks are on grain. Stitch over the pulled thread while holding the fabric taut. The bobbin thread draws the two needle threads together, creating the tuck. Place the first tuck under a channel of the pin-tuck foot to stitch additional tucks. The distance between tucks is determined by the channel selection on the pin-tuck foot. Be sure to stitch all pin tucks in the same direction.

I don't like to press pin tucks flat, so I place the tucks, right side down, on a soft, terry-cloth towel and gently steam from the wrong side. I don't allow the full weight of the iron to crush the tucks. To press between areas of tucks on the right side, I place one set of tucks off the edge of the ironing board and iron up to the next set.

Gathering—Controlling fullness with gathers requires some special techniques. Although one row of gathering stitches will work, I get better results with two rows.

Begin by stitching two gathering rows, ¼ in. and ⅛ in. from the edge; using 12 to 14 stitches per inch (drawing at right, above). The short stitches result in tiny gathers in the fine fabric. Then roll and whip the raw edge over the closest stitching line. Pull the bobbin thread to gather

and join to other garment pieces, using a conventional machine roll-and-whip technique or a serged rolled-hem seam. You can also use a small French seam. Curved seams are possible if the seam is narrow, the curves are gentle, and the gathers aren't too bulky.

Caring for your heirloom

Hand washing is appropriate for all fabrics, including wools; just remember to use a water temperature appropriate to the fiber and a soap product like Ivory. If a bleach is necessary, use an oxygen bleach, available at drugstores. Snowy Bleach is an example of a commercial oxygen bleach. Rinse until the water is completely clear. Any soap residue will break down the fibers and cause discoloration when the fabric is ironed. For stains, a laundry stick called Magic Wand, manufactured by Edwards Creative Products, gives good results. Rub it on directly from the tube, or gently work it in with a dampened, soft toothbrush.□

Carol Neumann is a home economist and former editor of the Singer Sewing Reference Library sewing books.

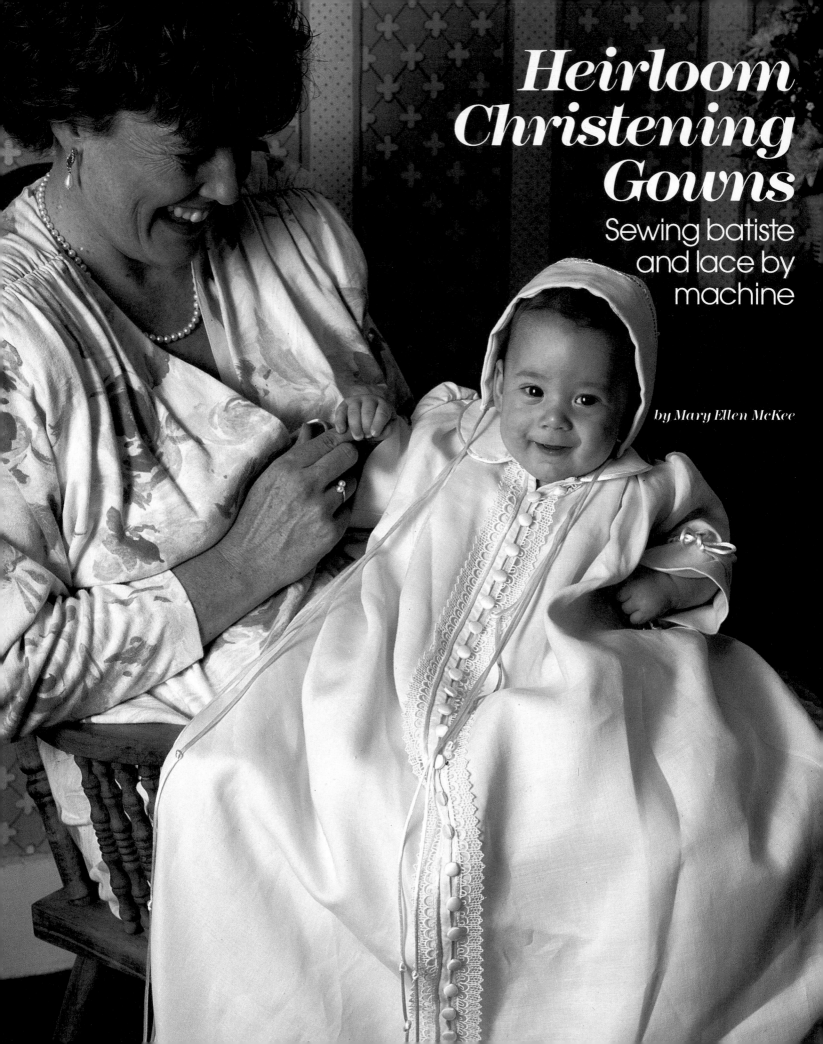

Heirloom Christening Gowns

Sewing batiste and lace by machine

by Mary Ellen McKee

during the Victorian era, parents doted on their children, often expressing this attitude by dressing the children grandly. It is not surprising that the Victorian infant gown was a showcase for the fine heirloom hand sewing that peaked during the late 19th century. These gowns replaced the traditional swaddling clothes with long flowing skirts, often a yard and a half long. The skirts, yokes, and sleeves were usually embellished with ribbons, laces, inserts, puffing, and many kinds of intricate embroidery. The techniques identified with hand sewing (rolling and whipping, puffing) were all combined in the child's dress.

This fashion has come down to us in the form of the christening gown. No longer everyday dress, the gown is special-occasion wear, reserved for one of the child's first public ceremonies. I make my christening gowns so that proud parents can have an heirloom to pass along and begin a family tradition.

Making a gown like the one pictured on the facing page takes between 25 and 50 hours of sewing. I recommend that you begin early, long before the arrival and demands of the baby, to allow plenty of time to make your gown.

Gather the right materials

The most important parts of an heirloom christening gown are the fabrics and laces. Choose these with a baby in mind, remembering that heavy satin looks wonderful on the bolt, but will be too stiff to suit your purpose.

My favorite fabrics for gowns are 100% cotton Swiss batiste and pure linen. These are long-wearing, washable fabrics, and excellent choices for a one-of-a-kind heirloom gown or robe. See Sources, on p. 34, for places to buy these fabrics and my favorite trims by mail order.

All-cotton batiste is available in several weights and finishes. Biaressima is a batiste with the highest available thread count with about 130 threads per inch, so it has the finest texture. Finella is lightweight and has a shiny, silklike texture. Nelona is a medium-weight fabric with less sheen than finella. Finissima has a matte finish and is heavier than the other batistes. Lightweight Irish linen feels soft on baby's skin but has a

The grandest labor of love: Put your finest details into a gown to be cherished for generations, and do it by machine. The outfit shown on the facing page is an example of modern heirloom sewing. (Photo by Susan Kahn)

more definite texture than the cottons. It looks especially nice when made into boys' gowns or contemporary designs.

Trims are usually classified as "Swiss" or "French," although these designations don't necessarily reflect the place of origin. Swiss trims are generally embroidered cotton. The finer, more delicate laces shown at top right in the photo on p. 34 are French.

Swiss or French trim that has two straight edges is called *insertion*. Insertion is meant to be sewn between two other edges, either between fabric pieces or between other trims. *Beading* is insertion made with a row of holes in the center for threading a ribbon through. *Edging*, trim that is straight on one side and shaped on the other, is meant to finish off the outermost edge of the cuff, skirt, or other piece being decorated.

One of the most commonly used trims in heirloom sewing is *entredeux*, shown in the upper drawings on p. 34. The literal translation is "between two," and that describes its use. Sewn between fabric and lace, entredeux makes a row of regular holes resembling hemstitching and forms a border for the lace. Entredeux comes in several sizes; the smallest is suitable for baby wear, the largest can be used as beading. For christening gowns, I use the size that has 14 holes per inch.

Ribbons, ribbon roses, and decorative closures are other possibilities for embellishing your gown. I recommend double-faced satin ribbon because it looks the same on both sides and is easy to work with. Ribbons can be used as streamers, made into roses as shown in the right-hand drawing on p. 35, and used for ties at the back of the dress or slip as an alternative to buttons or snaps. Another alternative is the beauty pin. These tiny clasps come in several shapes and finishes and are a classic way to complement an heirloom garment.

Finding a pattern or adapting your own

The christening gown is a simple, basic style. The luxury lies in embellishing the simple cut with trims and heirloom sewing techniques like puffs and tucks. While there are several commercial patterns on the market (nearly every pattern company has at least one, and Folkwear will be reissuing their vintage pattern by the end of the year), you can adapt an infant dress pattern very easily. Choose a newborn-sized pattern with a square or round yoke and puffed sleeves. You will need to lengthen the dress to about a 40-in. to 42-in. finished length for an antique gown. Contemporary ones

are shorter, sometimes only 20 inches. The skirt can vary in fullness from 40 in. at the bottom for shorter gowns to more than 100 in. in the very long antique styles. The average for commercial patterns is about 64 in. The light weight of the batiste makes it easy to gather this volume of fabric into the yoke.

Fabrics from trims—The essence of heirloom sewing is combining the laces and fabrics to make a design unlike anyone else's. Choose trims appropriate to the color and weight of your fabric. A very sheer batiste needs a delicate touch and may be overwhelmed by some of the Swiss trims. Try combining white trims with cream or ecru fabric. The contrast may please you.

You can also combine insertions to create original fabrics. I often use this method to make the bodice of the gown, since I can use small amounts of the same trim that I have chosen for the skirt to unify the dress. The left-hand drawing on p. 35 shows how to make a bonnet using edgings, insertions, beading, and ribbons.

The long, full skirt of the christening gown is the place to put your most elaborate work. Tuck the skirt with blind tucks above a flounce to give the bottom of the skirt some body. Set insertions into the fabric down the center front, forming a decorative panel to set off puffs or pin tucks. Make your own fabric from lace and set a wide band around the skirt. You can use these techniques alone or in combinations.

Use entredeux any time you sew lace to fabric. Choose a small entredeux and set your zigzag stitch width and length as shown in the drawing at the top of p. 34.

Machine gathers—In heirloom sewing by hand, the skirt is rolled, whipped, and gathered in one step. To gather by machine, you have some options. You can finish the top edge of the skirt with a zigzag stitch, setting your tensions to get the result shown in the top right drawing on p. 34. If you stitch over a gathering thread, you can pull up the thread when you've finished stitching. You can use your serger to finish the raw skirt edge, and some sergers allow the option of serging over a cord, giving the same result as the zigzag. You can also finish the edge, then gather it with straight hand or machine stitches in the seam allowance.

Sleeves may be long or short. Puffed sleeves look best with the antique style of the dress and are easy to fit over little wiggling hands. I cut my sleeves double, placing the hemline on a crosswise fold

Trims make the gown, as this photo of Mary Ellen McKee's work shows. The bonnet and dress from the same Swiss laces display Victorian elegance, while the gown at far left, made from resewn lace motifs, is more contemporary. The gowns are adapted from Vogue 2878. The gold beauty pins (upper right) make a dainty closure for either style. Also shown are entredeux and French laces (upper right), and a traditional prayer doll (lower left).

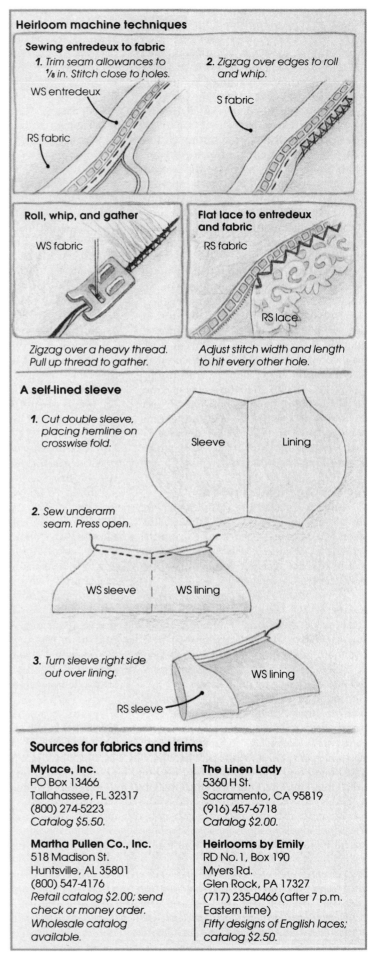

Heirloom machine techniques

Sewing entredeux to fabric

1. *Trim seam allowances to ⅛ in. Stitch close to holes.*

WS entredeux

RS fabric

2. *Zigzag over edges to roll and whip.*

S fabric

Roll, whip, and gather

WS fabric

Zigzag over a heavy thread. Pull up thread to gather.

Flat lace to entredeux and fabric

RS fabric

RS lace

Adjust stitch width and length to hit every other hole.

A self-lined sleeve

1. *Cut double sleeve, placing hemline on crosswise fold.*

Sleeve   Lining

2. *Sew underarm seam. Press open.*

WS sleeve   WS lining

3. *Turn sleeve right side out over lining.*

WS lining

RS sleeve

Sources for fabrics and trims

Mylace, Inc.
PO Box 13466
Tallahassee, FL 32317
(800) 274-5223
Catalog $5.50.

Martha Pullen Co., Inc.
518 Madison St.
Huntsville, AL 35801
(800) 547-4176
Retail catalog $2.00; send check or money order. Wholesale catalog available.

The Linen Lady
5360 H St.
Sacramento, CA 95819
(916) 457-6718
Catalog $2.00.

Heirlooms by Emily
RD No. 1, Box 190
Myers Rd.
Glen Rock, PA 17327
(717) 235-0466 (after 7 p.m. Eastern time)
Fifty designs of English laces; catalog $2.50.

of the fabric, as shown in the bottom drawing on the facing page. I sew the underarm seam from one end to the other and press seam allowances open. Then I turn the sleeve right side out over the lining, sandwiching the seam allowances between them. This produces a sleeve with no raw edges on the inside.

Trim the tiny sleeves with lace, perhaps using beading and a ribbon to gather the sleeve at the wrist or upper arm. This is easier to adjust, as baby gets chubbier, than elastic would be.

My favorite slip and the extras

The Little Vogue pattern I often use (No. 2878) includes a slip, but some patterns don't. You can modify your gown pattern by cutting the front and back neck edges ½ in. lower and adding ribbon ties to close the back, making a slip that can be used as sleepwear long after the christening. I often make the slip so the lace on the bottom shows below the hem of the gown. The other laces and trims on the slip will rarely be seen but will add to the lavishness of the outfit.

To complete the christening outfit, trim a 45-in. square of batiste or satin with ribbons and lace to make a blanket. Make fabric from lace as shown below, and use it for a fancy bonnet.

Storage and care hints

After the christening, you'll want to preserve your heirloom gown for the next generation. Before storing, be sure to remove all soil. Use a mild soap and warm water to clean any spots. Hold a clean, dry cloth under the garment while dabbing the right side with a cloth dipped in soapy water. When the soap has removed the stain, replace the under-cloth with a dry one and rinse by dabbing with clear water. If the gown is heavily soiled, you may want to hand wash it. Use a gentle soap like Ivory flakes, and rinse thoroughly. Lay the garment flat and allow it to dry completely before storing. The delicate fabrics and laces may not stand up to drip drying or tumbling in a machine.

Mary Lou Odle, Kansas State University Salina County Extension Agent, suggests that you store your gown in a cardboard box large enough to hold it without folding. Line the box with freshly washed unbleached muslin and wrap the gown in muslin or acid-free tissue paper, making sure the gown does not touch any part of the box. Store the box in a cool, dry storage room. Once a year, take the gown out of the box and check carefully for any damage. If you had to fold the gown to fit the box, rearrange the folds every year to avoid yellowing and weakening of the fabric on the crease lines. Wash and dry the muslin thoroughly, rewrap the gown, and store it away carefully for another year. □

Mary Ellen McKee of Salina, Kansas, makes her christening gowns and robes while listening to music in her loft studio. For information about special orders and custom-made materials kits which are tailored to individual taste, call her at (913) 823-7659, or write to Mary Ellen at 15 Red Fox La., Salina, KS 67401.

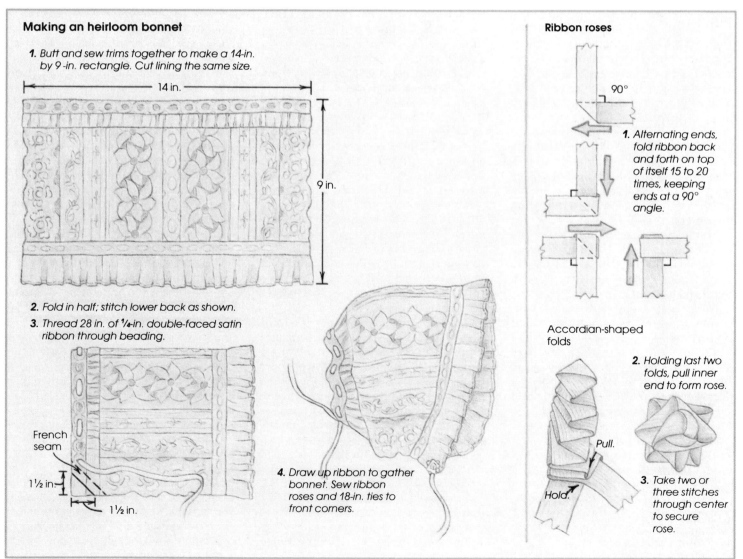

Making an heirloom bonnet

1. Butt and sew trims together to make a 14-in. by 9-in. rectangle. Cut lining the same size.

14 in.

9 in.

2. Fold in half; stitch lower back as shown.

3. Thread 28 in. of ¼-in. double-faced satin ribbon through beading.

French seam

1½ in.

1½ in.

4. Draw up ribbon to gather bonnet. Sew ribbon roses and 18-in. ties to front corners.

Ribbon roses

90°

1. Alternating ends, fold ribbon back and forth on top of itself 15 to 20 times, keeping ends at a 90° angle.

Accordian-shaped folds

2. Holding last two folds, pull inner end to form rose.

Pull.

Hold.

3. Take two or three stitches through center to secure rose.

Illustrations by Christine Charbonneau

Embellishment makes the outfit: Decorative machine stitching in white adds just the right amount of highlight to this crisp handkerchief linen blouse sewn from Butterick 5926. Two rows of a delicate hemstitch pattern, now found on many computerized machines, create a lacy pattern of open spaces.

Photo by Susan Kahn

A Simple Machine Embellishment

A delicate decorative hem is as close as your sewing machine

by Carol Laflin Ahles

these days many sewing machines have built-in decorative stitches that can create rows of finely embroidered holes, an airy effect that's often called hemstitching. I find that a lot of home sewers own machines with these stitches but aren't fully aware of how to use them. Here are two of my favorite stitches. They're versatile and easy to apply, whether to a garment in progress or to personalize the collar, cuffs, or hem of a purchased garment.

The two hemstitches that I use the most, called Parisian and Venetian, both create a pattern of delicate open spaces by automatically sewing in and out of the same holes many times. With the right needles and thread, which I'll describe in a bit, you can add an heirloom look, as I did on the outfit shown on the facing page, without the frills of lace, ruffles, and puffing.

Sewing machine options

When I began teaching machine hemstitching, in 1982, only a few sewing machines (most notably the electronic Elna with discs) had any usable hemstitches. Now there are many computer machines on the market that have hemstitches built in. (If you don't own a machine with these built-in stitches, you can still achieve the look of hemstitching with a two-row straight-stitch technique, as shown on p. 38.)

The Parisian stitch, shown in the diagram at left below, resembles the hand pin stitch (see pp. 40-41), which is used in heirloom sewing to stitch hems decoratively, as well as to attach and accent the edges of lace and appliqué. The Venetian stitch, shown at right below, can look like entredeux, a narrow machine-embroidered trim with a ladder of open holes that's often used in heirloom sewing. Using the Venetian stitch, you can create the effect of entredeux while you hem, attach lace, or topstitch.

To locate the Parisian and Venetian stitches on your sewing machine, compare the stitch diagrams below to the drawings in your machine manual. The path the needle actually follows to make the stitches varies among sewing machine companies and models.

Some machines have a picot stitch, which traces the same pattern as the Parisian without repeating any part of it. You can use the picot stitch in place of the Parisian, but the single-stitched holes will not be as distinct.

Big needle, small thread

For perfect machine stitching, you usually match the thread and needle size, but airy hemstitching is an exception to this rule. A fine thread sewn with a large universal or wing needle (see *Threads* No. 48, p. 18) creates the most distinct holes.

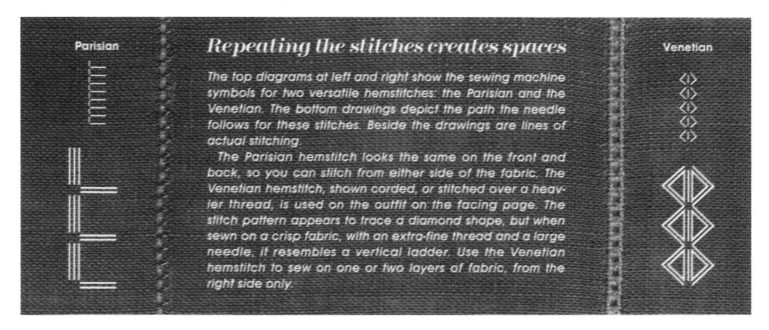

Parisian

Venetian

Repeating the stitches creates spaces

The top diagrams at left and right show the sewing machine symbols for two versatile hemstitches: the Parisian and the Venetian. The bottom drawings depict the path the needle follows for these stitches. Beside the drawings are lines of actual stitching.

The Parisian hemstitch looks the same on the front and back, so you can stitch from either side of the fabric. The Venetian hemstitch, shown corded, or stitched over a heavier thread, is used on the outfit on the facing page. The stitch pattern appears to trace a diamond shape, but when sewn on a crisp fabric, with an extra-fine thread and a large needle, it resembles a vertical ladder. Use the Venetian hemstitch to sew on one or two layers of fabric, from the right side only.

From *Threads* magazine (August 1993) 48:52-55

Fine threads—An all-purpose sewing thread tends to fill up the holes, so they don't look as open. For best results, use a good-quality extra-fine cotton machine-embroidery thread such as Madeira size 80/2, Mettler size 60/2, or DMC size 50/2 (for sources, see the facing page).

You can match the thread color to the fabric for a subtle look, or use contrasting thread for more definition. With the Venetian stitch, a contrasting thread looks best corded (stitched over a heavier thread) in the same color, as shown on p. 36. (See "Cording the stitch" on the facing page.)

Large needles—For the best effect, you should choose a needle that's large enough to create a hole, but not so large as to distort the fabric. I recommend a size 100 wing needle for heavy fabrics such as cotton piqué and some linens. On finer fabrics such as handkerchief linen, an extra-large size 120/19 universal needle is less likely to cause puckering or damage. For delicate Swiss cotton batiste, I may use a size 100/16 universal needle or even smaller. For the extra-large universal and wing needles, try your sewing machine dealer or the sources on the facing page.

Selecting fabric and a pattern

Knowing the appropriate fabric choices and pattern styles makes good hemstitching results easier to obtain. Stable fabric is the key. To add crispness and body, use spray starch or a tear-away stabilizer.

Fabric—Decorative hemstitching works best on a woven fabric with body; the repeated stitching with a large needle can draw up and distort a softer fabric. I suggest fabrics with a high percentage of linen or cotton and little or no polyester, such as linen and cotton organdy. Many fabrics can be spray-starched and pressed to add body and crispness. Repeated light to medium applications of spray starch, alternated with pressing, will build up body and minimize scorching.

Sometimes an unlikely fiber content or fabric texture gives surprisingly good results. For example, 51 percent acetate, 49 percent cotton faille moiré adapts beautifully to hemstitching. And relatively bumpy Swiss cotton piqué works consistently well. When in doubt, try stitching on a sample of fabric.

Stabilizers—If a fabric puckers even with spray starch, try stitching over one or two layers of a lightweight tear-away stabilizer, which gives the fabric more body. After stitching, carefully tear or cut away the excess stabilizer. Jiffy Tear Away from Staple and both Soft and Stiff from Speed Stitch all work well. For sources, see the facing page.

Choosing a pattern—Most patterns designed for cotton/linen fabrics can be embellished with a hemstitching effect. It's easy to add decorative stitching on the crosswise grain of the fabric, such as on a cuff, pocket, or straight hem. Stitching on the lengthwise grain, curves, and bias lines can result in distortion if the fabric has not been stabilized adequately.

Experimenting with built-in hemstitches

Before attempting to apply decorative stitching to a garment, it's important to test and adjust the materials, tools, and machine settings to get the best-looking stitch. If you make well-labeled samples, they will serve as a helpful reference each time you sew with hemstitching.

Assemble scraps of fabrics such as linen, linen/cotton blends, and organdy (inexpensive domestic organdy is fine for testing). Spray-starch and iron to make the swatches crisp.

With a size 100/16 wing or 120/19 universal needle and extra-fine thread, stitch a sample of each hemstitch on single and double layers of the various fabrics.

Feet, stitch width, and length—For the Parisian hemstitch, I use an ordinary zigzag presser foot and a stitch width and length of 2 to 2.5 mm for the look of hand pin stitching. The Venetian hemstitch usually works best with a satin stitch or embroidery foot; the groove on the underside of the foot allows for the buildup

Sewing a hemstitch with straight stitches requires two passes of stitching with a double-wing needle. Note that the double-wing actually has one regular universal point and one broad, flat wing needle. The wing needle makes a large hole. After stitching one row with the wing needle making a large hole, rotate the fabric 180 degrees and stitch a second row, overlapping the first, with the wing needle hitting in the same holes it created on the first row.

A hemstitched look from a basic machine

If you don't own a machine that has built-in hemstitches, you can still create beautiful decorative hems on your garments and linens. The two-row straight-stitch technique, sewn with a double-wing needle (one regular needle and one wing needle) as shown in the photo above, works on most sewing machines that can use twin needles. (To check, install the double needle and zigzag throat plate and turn the handwheel toward you one full turn to make sure the needles don't strike your machine's throat plate or hook.) You can use the two-row straight stitch as a decorative stitch or to edge a hem sewn through two layers. Afterwards, you can trim the underlayer close to the stitching.

As you would with the built-in stitches, I suggest making some samples to practice the stitch. Follow the suggestions under "Selecting fabric and a pattern," above, to choose an appropriate fabric, and apply spray starch for crispness. With a size 100 double-wing needle and extra-fine thread, stitch one row with the stitch length set to medium, about 2 to 2.5 mm. Adjust the upper thread tension to give enough pull to open the holes, but not so much as to cause puckering. At the end of the first row, lift the needles and presser foot and turn the fabric 180 degrees. Then stitch a second partially overlapping row, so that only the wing needle hits precisely the same holes as it made on the first row, as shown in the photo above. Sewing slowly on the second row gives you more control over the precise stitch placement.

To make it easier to see and enter the previous row of holes exactly, use a presser foot that allows visibility, such as a transparent plastic foot or an open-toe embroidery/satin stitch foot.

Making sure the needle hits exactly into the holes that it made on the first row can be tedious, but with practice you will produce a beautiful hemstitching effect. *–C.A.*

Balancing the stitch: At left, the Venetian stitch before and after balancing, which corrects alignment so repeating stitches hit in the same holes. A jagged mass of stitches becomes a decorative pattern.

When sewing the Venetian stitch over two strands of cord (below), the large holes form in the center, between cords. The V-shaped stitches to the left and right cross over the cords. A foot with grooves or holes helps to keep the strands the correct distance apart.

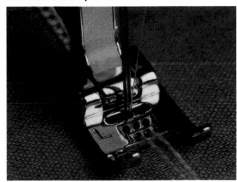

of stitches. Experiment with a stitch width of 3 to 3.7 mm and a length of 2.5 mm, if the length is adjustable on your sewing machine.

Tension—Increasing the upper thread tension slightly will tighten the stitching, which will make the holes larger. However, too much tension can cause puckering. If you're happy with the upper thread tension, but you still have puckering on a well-starched fabric, try using a stabilizer underneath.

Balancing the stitch—For beautiful hemstitching, it's important that the needle hit precisely in the same holes as it repeats parts of the stitch pattern. If the hemstitch holes on your sample do not look distinct or if stray threads cross the holes, experiment with the balance or fine adjustment of the stitch, if your machine has this feature (see the photo above left).

Many factors affect the stitch alignment, such as the kind of fabric you use, the number of layers of fabric, the grain direction, and the stabilizer you choose. For example, if a fabric draws up slightly, the repeat stitches will not hit in the same hole. The balancing feature lengthens or shortens the forward or backward stitches within a stitch pattern to bring the parts of the pattern into alignment. This can make a big difference in the appearance of the stitch, as shown in the photo above left. Not all machines have this feature, so consult your manual. Be sure to include any balancing adjustments in your swatch notes.

Cording the stitch

To add definition, color, and stability to a line of hemstitching, you can add cording. Use one strand of cord with the Parisian hemstitch, so the horizontal stitch sews over it. With the Venetian stitch, use two strands of cord so the left side of the stitch crosses over the left cord, and the right side crosses the right cord, with the large holes forming in the center between the cords, as in the photo above right. The cord emphasizes the vertical lines and makes the hemstitching more visible.

Selecting a cord—You can choose from different sizes of cord, depending on the weight of the fabric and the effect you want. For a heavy fabric such as cotton piqué, try cording with size 5 pearl cotton. On handkerchief linen, I cord with a lighter size 8 pearl cotton. Cotton cords are available at local stores or from the sources above. You can also experiment with buttonhole twist and topstitching threads as lighter cords for hemstitching. On a fine Swiss batiste, I cord with four strands of thread for a delicate effect.

Feet—It's helpful to have a presser foot that guides the cord, either one with grooves on the bottom or, even better, one with a choice of holes. Experiment with your machine's traditional buttonhole foot or a special foot with holes, such as Elna's Multiple-Cord Sole (with five or seven holes) or Viking's 7-Hole Cording Foot. You can also use an embroidery or satin-stitch foot, and sew with a strand of cord on each side of the needle.

Exploring applications

You can use the Parisian or the Venetian stitch on a single layer of fabric, or on a double layer such as a single-fold hem, a placket, or a garment and its facing. For sewing on a double layer of fabric, stitch through both layers, staying ½ in. away from any raw edge; then trim the raw edge close to the stitching. The Parisian stitch also works well next to a folded edge such as a double-fold hem or a tuck, or next to a finished edge such as ribbon or trim, so that the forward-and-backward stitches of the pattern fall on a single layer of fabric and the horizontal stitch catches the fold or trim. The Venetian stitch is not usually sewn over a folded edge, because it's difficult to get good results.

Besides hems and decorative topstitching, you'll find many other uses for the versatile Parisian and Venetian stitches. Use either stitch to attach rows or shapes of lace to fabric. With the Venetian stitch, you can create faggoting, which is a decorative stitching over an open space between two separate pieces of fabric or lace. Try using the Parisian stitch for delicate appliquéing or with a 2- to 4-mm narrow hemming foot for an elegant narrow hem. These exciting techniques invite experimentation and can add just the right amount of embellishment to a simple garment. □

Carol Laflin Ahles, a former sewing machine dealer in Houston, TX, writes and teaches classes on machine hemstitching and other heirloom sewing techniques throughout the United States.

Pin-stitching creates a line of decorative holes while attaching lace to fabric. The fabric is trimmed after stitching.

The Joys of French Handsewing

Hand stitches preserve the drape of fine fabrics and delicate laces

by Regina Madory Walter

as knitters often do, I've enjoyed using long train or plane rides to make a garment. Except I don't knit; I sew. If this sounds appealing, you might like to try French handsewing, so called because it is believed to have originated with French nuns. I became fascinated with fine French handsewn blouses and lingerie from the Victorian era, and took up French handsewing with a passion.

Fine French handsewing creates delicate, beautiful garments that are comfortable, washable, and durable. The finished piece, whether a pillow, a blouse (see the photo on the facing page), or an intricate christening dress, becomes a treasured heirloom. A project like a Swiss cotton batiste blouse trimmed with lace is relaxing to work on and folds into a purse to carry wherever you go. It's the only type of garment sewing I can do on a plane or train, in a car, or at the beach, completing components at odd moments—ten minutes here, twenty minutes there.

Many people enjoy doing heirloom sewing by machine. The interlocking threads of machine stitching, however, stiffen fine fabrics such as batiste and lawn. Sewing these fabrics by hand results in a rich softness that machines cannot duplicate.

The heirloom pillow shown on p. 43 makes an elegant birth or wedding gift and is a good introduction to some of the basic techniques. You can also practice on an uncomplicated blouse, using the basics plus pin stitching, shown above and on the facing page. I suggest a blouse pattern especially designed for heirloom sewing (see "Sources" on p. 42).

Selecting materials

The inside of a French handsewn garment or pillow is as beautifully finished as the outside, with no raw edges. Tiny seams between fabric and lace or fabric and fabric (such as an armhole seam) are rolled and whipped onto a thin, openwork trim called *entredeux* (more about this in a bit). Less visible areas such as side and underarm seams are sewn together with narrow French seams (see *Threads* No. 45, p. 16). Since the fabrics used are sheer or semi-transparent, the construction techniques enhance the finished piece.

Fabrics appropriate for French handsewing include Swiss cotton batiste and organdy, cotton dotted Swiss, handkerchief linen, and silk batiste, organza, and chiffon, available from local fabric stores or from the mail-order sources listed on p. 42. (For definitions and descriptions of these fabrics, see *Threads* No. 45, p. 16.) I suggest cotton batiste for a first project, since it's the easiest to sew.

To complement these fine fabrics, I prefer to use French cotton laces and Swiss

From *Threads* magazine (February 1993) 45:62-65

A lacy line of stitching

Pin stitching, which forms a line of decorative holes, can attach fabric to fabric, fabric to lace, or lace to lace.

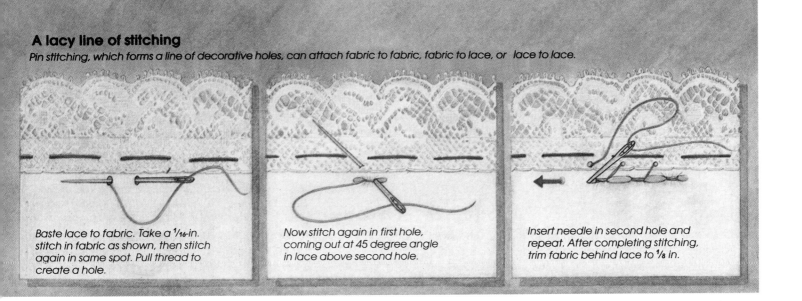

Baste lace to fabric. Take a 1/16-in. stitch in fabric as shown, then stitch again in same spot. Pull thread to create a hole.

Now stitch again in first hole, coming out at 45 degree angle in lace above second hole.

Insert needle in second hole and repeat. After completing stitching, trim fabric behind lace to 1/8 in.

Garmentmaking can be an ideal activity on a long plane or train trip, if you apply French handsewing techniques. Sew a project like the batiste blouse at right in manageable sections, then assemble. The handsewn pillow shown on p. 43 is a way to get started.

embroidered trims. Both are available in several coordinating styles, including *edging* (with one shaped edge), *insertion* (with two straight edges), *beading* (with holes for lacing a ribbon), *galloon* (wider, with two shaped edges), and *medallions*, or free-standing lace motifs. You can match or mix different trim patterns in one project. Many fine laces are now made of 90 percent cotton with 10 percent nylon for strength, and they require a cool iron to prevent melting and holes.

Always buy extra lace and trims for turning corners, shaping curves, and matching motifs and edge scallops. For gathered areas, such as the ruffle with lace edging on the pillow shown on p. 43, I allow at least a two-to-one ratio of ruffle to edge, for the correct fullness.

Entredeux, which means "between two," is a trim used extensively in French handsewing to join fabric to fabric and fabric to lace, adding stability to the seam

Photo by Susan Kahn

Roll and whip the edge of fabric lace:
1. Moisten your left thumb, grasp the left edge of the fabric, and roll the edge along the side of your index finger far enough for one or two stitches. Create tension on the fabric by holding the right end in your right fingers.

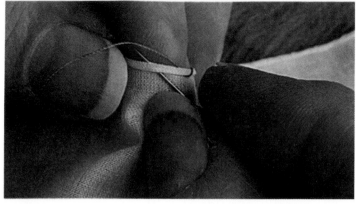

2. To whip, hold the roll over your left index finger as shown in the photo above. Insert the needle under (not through) the roll, and emerge on the edge at a 45 degree angle. Repeat for several stitches, wrapping the roll with thread. The thread doesn't show on the right side. (Pastel thread used for demonstration only.)

A puffing strip starts out the same as rolling and whipping: Just pull the whipping thread to gather the strip edges, creating soft waves. Gather to the length of strips you need.

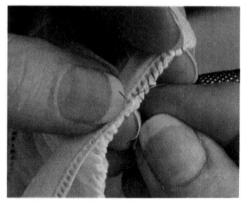

Stitching a puffing strip to entredeux: Place the puffing strip and the entredeux right sides together. Whip the edges together, one stitch per hole, catching the entire roll.

---

and preventing stretch. Made by machine stitching on fine batiste to form a ladder, the best quality entredeux comes from Switzerland, in a variety of widths. I usually use ⅛-in.-wide entredeux, and trim away the batiste before whipping, one side at a time.

Extra-fine 100 percent cotton sewing thread, such as Swiss-Metrosene embroidery thread size 60/2, and tiny needles (size 10 or 12 betweens), both available from the sources at right, enable the sewer to control the small running stitches that are used in French seams. Run the thread through beeswax twice for strength and easier stitching. It's best to avoid knots, which tend to show through the fabric. Instead, anchor all threads with tiny running stitches, back stitches, or with a quilters' knot (see *Threads* No. 44, p. 16).

Lace stretches easily, so it's important to measure, cut, and sew it in a relaxed, unstretched state. Comparing the work to a paper template while stitching helps prevent distortion.

Using these techniques, you can make a wide variety of keepsakes from clothing to bed and table linens, or, if you're very ambitious, even a wedding gown! □

Regina Madory Walter lives in Annandale, VA, and teaches fine handsewing workshops throughout the United States.

Sources

Fabrics, trims, books, and patterns for heirloom sewing are available from:

G Street Fabrics
11854 Rockville Pike
Rockville, MD 20852
(301) 231-8960

Margaret Pierce, Inc.
PO Box 4542
Greensboro, NC 27404
(919) 292-6430
Catalog $2.

Calico House
Rte. 4, Box 16
Scottsville, VA 24590
(804) 286-2979

Creating an elegant pillow

The 12-in. pillow on the facing page offers practice for a few French handsewing techniques. The strips of fabric and lace are sewn together along their straight grains. The pillow edges, however, fall on the bias, so you'll need to check the squareness of the pillow against a paper template as you proceed. To create a template, draw a 13-in. square (includes ½-in. seam allowances) on paper, then draw four lines to bisect it vertically, horizontally, and diagonally. As you work, check that each added strip of trim or fabric extends beyond the template's edges; you'll trim the pillow before you add the ruffle. The fabric layout is shown on the facing page.

1 To begin, straighten one end of the batiste by pulling a thread (see Threads No. 45, p. 16) and cutting on the line. Then pull a thread to cut each section of the pillow exactly on grain, following the diagram on the facing page. Mark the horizontal and vertical centers of the center panel and the horizontal center of each puffing strip with lines of basting in a contrasting pastel thread.

2 Join the short ends of the three pieces of the ruffle with French seams to form a circle. Roll and whip one side (see the instructions at top left), then whip lace edging to the rolled edge, right sides together.

3 On the center panel, draw or trace a design and embroider, if desired. Roll and whip the long sides, then whip entredeux to each side.

4 Whip lace insertion, then entredeux, then lace beading to each side of the center panel. Note: many laces look best if you line up or alternate the lace motifs.

5 Draw a 2-in.-wide paper strip as long as the edge of the center panel for a template. Draw horizontal

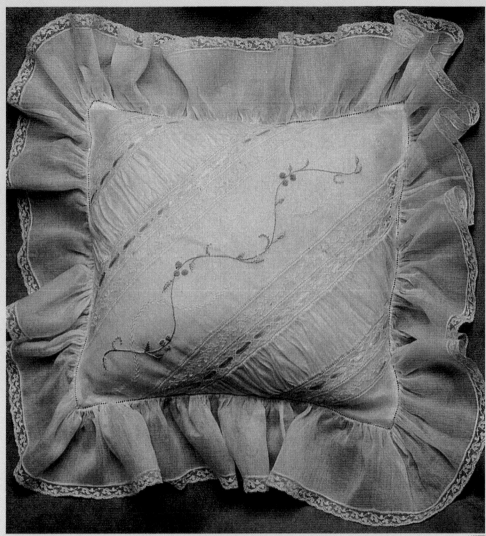

A soft, French handsewn pillow combines imported fabric and lace using just a few fine handsewing techniques, such as rolling and whipping edges to lace, and gathering a puffing strip (see the photos on the facing page for these techniques).

and vertical center lines on the paper. Pin the ends of a puffing strip to the template, then roll and whip the long sides with waxed thread. Pull up gathers, matching centers of the strip and template. Whip entredeux to each side.

6 Whip a puffing strip to each side of the center panel, lining up the centers of panel and puffing strips. To the puffing strip edge, add lace beading, a row of entredeux, a strip of lace insertion, and a final row of entredeux.

7 Place the pillow top on the 13-in template and cut two rectangles of batiste for the corner sections. Roll and whip one 6-in. edge, then whip to the panel.

8 Thread ribbon through the beading and tack it to the panel on the pillow seamline.

9 The back is made in two pieces that overlap in the center so you can insert the pillow. On one long edge of each back panel, fold under ¾ in., press, fold again, and stitch the hem in place. Place back panels on the template to form a square, right sides up. Baste the overlap in place along the seamlines.

10 Place the pillow top, right side down, over the back. Mark the seamline and trim the seam allowances to ½ In. Taking care not to stretch the top, sew the seam with tiny running stitches. Trim to ¼ In. and overcast.

11 Turn pillow and carefully press the edges. Whip entredeux to outer edge, catching just the seamline. At each corner, extend entredeux one hole past corner, cut, and overlap next side to form a right angle.

12 Mark the center of each pillow side. Divide the ruffle into quarters. Roll and whip the ruffle, then gather up to fit the sides of the top. Match marks and whip the ruffle to the entredeux, positioning the ruffle's French seams away from the pillow corners. Allow enough fullness at the corners to avoid cupping. —R.M.W.

Materials for the heirloom pillow

- ⅞ yd. Swiss batiste
- 5½ yds. entredeux
- 1½ yds. each:
  ⅝ in.-wide lace insertion
  ⅝-in.-wide lace beading and ribbon to fit beading
- 3½ yds. lace edging
- Fine cotton sewing thread, size 60/2
- Cotton embroidery floss

Fabric layout for heirloom pillow

Pull a thread to cut out each section for the pillow above, following the diagram below.

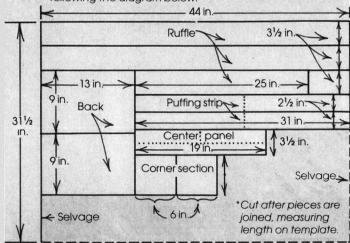

44 in.

Ruffle — 3½ in.

13 in. — 25 in.

9 in. Back

31½ in.

Puffing strip — 2½ in.

31 in.

Center panel — 3½ in.
19 in.

9 in.

Corner section

Selvage

Selvage — 6 in.

*Cut after pieces are joined, measuring length on template.

Illustrations by Marianne Markey

Decorative Stitching on Felted Fabric

Double-needle stitch patterns mimic intricate textured knitting

by Joy B. Landeira

boiled wool fabric has many wonderful qualities. It's warm, wrinkle-free, slightly stretchy, long wearing, and easy to sew, with no seam finishing, lining, or facing required. It looks woven, but it's actually a knit.

While experimenting with a double needle on my sewing machine (any zigzag machine with a 4mm-wide needle hole will work), I discovered that I could make textured ribs on boiled wool fabric by simply stitching over the fabric. The knit structure and the soft, thick loft of the felted wool yarns turn what would be simple pin tucks on ordinary fabric into dramatic raised welts.

I was even able to stitch corners with my double needle because I could pivot the fabric with the double needle down, without distorting the fabric or the stitch. The stretchy fabric simply absorbs the movement of the needle. Corners are usually impossible with thinner fabric, which greatly reduces the possible range of patterns you can sew with double needles. Boiled wool has enough give so that the needle won't break on most angles, even ones of 90 degrees or more.

So what can you do with this intriguing discovery? Since I love the traditional ribs, cables, diamonds, and geometrics of Irish fishermen's knits, I decided to use these as the inspiration for an overall sewn-in surface design to personalize my own version of the classic boiled wool jacket. I call the finished product, shown on the facing page, my "Austri-Aran Boiled Wool Jacket" since it combines the traditional princess cut of a cropped Austrian jacket with the surface design and color of Aran Isle fishermen's knits. Following is a description of the materials and steps I used to make it.

Assembling the ingredients

My heavyweight boiled wool fabric and matching braid is made by Landau Woolens. Your local fabric store may carry a few colors, although it's available in more than a dozen colors and in both medium and heavy weights by mail order (for a list of suppliers, see *Threads* No. 42, p. 82). If you want to make your own boiled wool, it's easier to start with a woven fabric. Pick a hand-loomed or store-bought open-weave wool, as described in *Threads* No. 42, p. 20. If you've got a wool afghan or big sweater that you've (accidentally) shrunk, you could cut it up and use that.

You'll also need folded woven braid to cover the edges at hem, cuff, neckline, and at the center-front opening. The mail-order sources listed usually have braid to match the yardage they sell. I use 100 percent polyester thread (I like Metrosene) or cotton-covered polyester thread in a matching color, but cotton or silk thread may work just as well. I use a Schmetz size 4.0 double needle, like the one in the drawing on the facing page. That's the smallest size that will work; they're widely available, or order by mail from Clotilde, 1909 S.W. First Ave., Fort Lauderdale, FL 33315; (800) 772-2891. For sewing seams, I use a size 80 or 90 universal or ballpoint needle. I find a quilting guide attachment useful for spacing the straight lines on the design panels, and I use a see-through ruler and a disappearing-ink marker for planning and marking the geometrics.

Choose a jacket pattern with simple lines and a minimum of gathers and darts. Princess styles, cardigans, and capes all work well in boiled wool. Eliminate facings and linings, choose pockets with minimum thickness (no welts!), and

avoid designs with zippers. If you want the look of cuffs or lapels, just turn back the braid-covered edge to expose the wrong side. In the traditional garments, turned-back details are often anchored with a button. Most pattern companies offer a traditionally styled jacket suitable for boiled wool.

Making preparations

Even though boiled wool has been thoroughly shrunk and felted to create the texture it now has, the manufacturer stretched and finished it to put it on the bolt, so it can still shrink as much as 20 percent. If you intend to hand wash the garment, which is a sensible alternative with unlined boiled wool, purchase ¼ to ½ yard extra fabric to allow for shrinkage, then soak your fabric and trims in warm water and roll them in a white terry-cloth towel to remove the excess water. Let the fabric lie flat until almost dry, then steam the wool, avoiding any direct pressure on the fabric surface, which might leave an imprint.

For garments that will be dry-cleaned, thoroughly steam the fabric and trim and let them dry fully before you cut. If you've created your own boiled wool, no further fabric preparation is necessary.

Preparing the pattern—I'd never plunge into such luxurious fabric without making a test garment to check the fit of the pattern, but I'm not one to use muslin for fittings, because when I'm done there's just a pile of muslin left. I made my trial garment out of an itchy royal blue wool-mohair remnant in my stash that had a loft similar to boiled wool. It turned out so well that I lined it to the edge with a printed cotton flannel to create an itch barrier, sandwiching blue knit piping

From *Threads* magazine (August 1992) 42:42-45

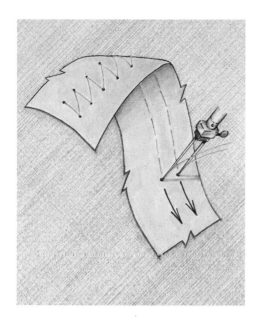

between the fabric and lining. Even the double-needle technique worked, as you can see in the photo on p. 47.

Once you have your pattern fine-tuned, it's worth spending some time to find an economical layout. First trim off any hem or seam allowances around the neckline, lapels, hems, and sleeve hems, since you'll be using braid at these edges. You should be able to cut a waist-length jacket out of 1¼ yards of 60-in.-wide boiled wool. It's important to align the major pattern pieces on the straight grain, but if your pattern has any small details, they can be cut off grain. One advantage of boiled wool is that there is no right or wrong side, so you may be able to flip a pattern piece over to fit in just the right spot. I cut only one fabric layer at a time, especially on the heavyweight wool. Use shears; the fabric is simply too thick and stretchy for rotary cutters.

Sewing double-needle pin tucks, or welts, into the fabric definitely pulls it in a little. To allow for this, I added an inch of extra ease to the side seams and sleeve edges of my Austri-Aran jacket. If you want to be extra cautious, add an inch all around the pattern pieces. Then, after decorating each piece, put it back on the pattern and recut to size.

Machine setup—A size 4.0 double needle is the only width that makes a suitable rib in the wool. Smaller widths or triple needles flatten the fabric, without sufficient width to make raised ribs. The bobbin thread forms a zigzag on the wrong side of the fabric, going between the stitches made by the top needles, as in the drawing above. If your machine starts to skip stitches or otherwise complains, try slowing down to allow the bobbin thread to do all this extra work. ⇨

Joy Landeira's textured jacket isn't knitted; it's made of boiled wool and machine embroidered with a double needle to create textured ribs and patterns that mimic fishermen's knits. (Photo by Susan Kahn)

Newer machines usually have two spool pins to accommodate two thread sources. If yours doesn't, wind an extra bobbin and place it and your thread spool together on the single pin. In either case, have one spool unwinding clockwise, and the other spool counterclockwise. Thread your machine as usual, passing the two threads together through all the loops and eyelets. But if your machine has a tension slot with a separating disk, arrange the threads to pass through on opposite sides of the disk, and thread each end through the eye of the needle on the corresponding side.

I use a 3.0mm stitch length or slightly longer, or about nine stitches to the inch, and normal tension for top and bobbin threads. If your welts aren't sticking up enough, try tightening the bobbin tension slightly.

For sewing seams and welts, I use a normal presser foot. You may find a satin-stitch embroidery foot with its channel underneath useful to accommodate the thickness of the welt. I use an attachable walking foot when sewing any kind of bias tape or double fold braid, on any fabric, and it makes attaching the braid on boiled wool a breeze, since it eliminates any bunching up. I set my machine for normal presser-foot pressure, but experiment with the tension if you're having trouble with the fabric feeding.

Stitching the designs

With the exception of the shoulder seams, as described on the facing page, I complete all the decorative double-needle stitching before doing any construction stitching. I staystitch all the curved seams, however, right after cutting out the pattern, to protect them from getting distorted.

To accentuate the styling of my Austri-Aran jacket, I decided not to do any decorative stitching on the side fronts or side backs, as you can see in the drawing below left. The princess seams are more evident this way, and I also didn't have to worry about matching the design over them or at the side seams. If I'd chosen a design without princess seams, I'd probably opt for an allover design.

Choosing stitch patterns—Experiment first on a fabric scrap to find patterns you like. On my jacket, I tried to choose symmetrical designs such as diamonds, cables, honeycombs, and zigzags that could be sewn in two continuous passes across the whole length of the pattern piece. This way I could stitch half the design, then go back and do the second half over it in a mirror image to complete the pattern.

I positioned my stitch patterns the same way as I would design an Aran sweater, by starting with a wide central panel and designing identical panels on each side for perfect symmetry. I decided to outline each new pattern with two straight ribs of double-needle stitching, as you can see in the close-up photo below. I varied the width of the panels as they moved away from the center, to keep the rhythm of the design interesting. I also varied the shapes (angles vs. curves) and sizes of motifs (large diamonds vs. small cables, etc.).

Once I had a design I liked, I planned simply to repeat it on each decorated pattern piece (the back, the sleeves, and two fronts), aligning the center of the design with the centers of the pieces, as in the drawing at left. The back and fronts were wider than the sleeves, so I added an extra panel of wide zigzag to fill up their extreme edges.

I duplicated the diamond panel at each center front so they would overlap, allowing the pattern to match across the front. I chose diamonds so I could place a button or buttonhole in the center of each diamond. To keep the braided edge finish from interrupting the design, I added the width of the braid to each center front, and started that far in when I made the first row of welt stitches.

To be absolutely sure of the design lines, you could mark all of the stitching lines on the fabric with a disappearing marker before sewing. But if you know you'll just be stitching straight from point to point, simply mark the points where the lines will cross (along the vertical center of the panels) and where they will hit the side ribs and change direction. Because the welt stitches gradually alter the

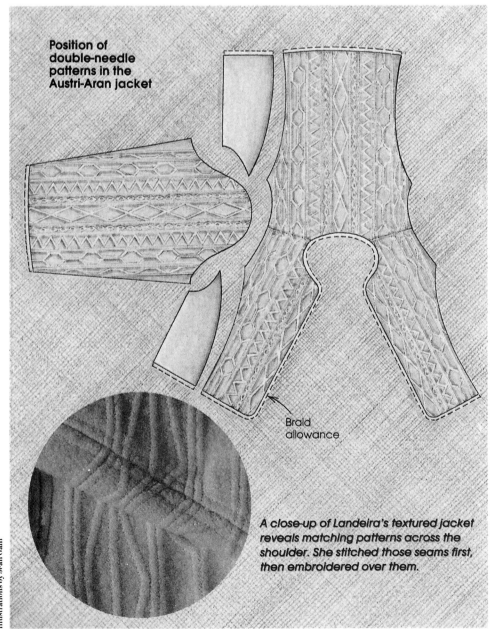

Position of double-needle patterns in the Austri-Aran jacket

Braid allowance

A close-up of Landeira's textured jacket reveals matching patterns across the shoulder. She stitched those seams first, then embroidered over them.

Illustrations by Jean Galli

dimensions of the fabric as you stitch, mark and stitch each panel before marking the adjacent one.

Decorative stitching the panels—Since all my designs were bounded on each side by straight ribs, I did these first. To make the ribs, stitch one straight line down the length of the pattern piece where you want the side of your center panel to be. Then place the left needle on top of the line previously stitched by the right needle and stitch beside the first welt, keeping the stitches directly on top of the previous ones. You'll end up with three lines of stitching forming a double rib.

To make the diamonds, I started at the center-top point (allowing for the width of the braid trim) and stitched to the first side marker on the outside edge of the panel. I left the double needle in the fabric at the marker, raised the presser foot, and repositioned the fabric to sew back across the center of the panel to the outside point on the next diamond. After sewing one side, I started again at the center top and stitched down for the other side of the diamonds. The cables on either side were so narrow that I decided to make the job easier by curving the stitching before I reached the outside point. I made a series of alternating curves, instead of zigzags, all the way down.

Stitching the shoulders—I completed each panel on all the pieces before going on to the next panel, working symmetrically out from the center panel. But when I came to the shoulders seams, I realized I'd have a hard time matching the patterns if I did front and back separately, so I decided to sew these seams first. I topstitched each seam on both sides ¼ in. from the pressed-open seam for a finish, trimmed the excess allowance, then redesigned the patterns slightly to go over the shoulder seam. The patterns didn't need to match at the armscyes, so I set in the sleeves after the texturing was done.

Construction and finishing—After sewing the seams, I finished all of them as just described for the shoulder seams. First I pressed them open using a tailors' ham to shape the princess seams, then I topstitched on each side of the seam. I trimmed off the excess seam allowance with the scissors angled sideways to bevel the cut so the edge would blend into the fabric beneath it.

You can finish the sleeves and all the outside edges with braid, Ultrasuede, or serged yarn trim. Braid that's been dyed to match needs only to be topstitched in place with matching thread. The braid's

Double-needle welts can take other forms. The Austrian crystal beaded stems at bottom were done on a woven fabric that resembles boiled wool. The hand embroidery in the pink jacket was made with yarn unraveled from dyed-to-match braid trim. Landeira's beret was embellished with welt-stitched reverse appliqué. She snipped away the top layer to reveal colored swatches underneath caught in the double-needle stitching.

raw edges can be lightly zigzagged over. I try to position the end joins at the side and underarm seams.

Machine-made buttonholes will definitely stretch, so be sure to stitch your buttonholes over a cord (see *Threads* No. 42, p. 18). I sew on buttons using a plastic backing button. Spray silver or pewter buttons with two layers of clear spray shellac to prevent tarnishing.

More design ideas

I've tried double-needle welt stitching on many fabrics that have a soft, thick, and flexible texture like boiled wool, and it usually works fine. One of my most successful experiments was on a purchased felted wool knit beret. I basted my collection of boiled wool swatches in a ring around the edge of the beret on the inside, and topstitched around them with a double needle from the outside. Then I cut away the beret layer to reveal the colored swatches underneath. You can see the results above. The raw edges haven't raveled yet.

To find the perfect matching wool yarn for embroidery on your boiled wool creation, like the example in the photo above, just unravel a leftover piece of the braid, which has already been dyed to match by the company. □

When she isn't sewing or teaching Spanish at the University of Colorado, Boulder, Joy Landeira restores Porsches and Corvettes.

Luxurious Lace

An expensive but forgiving fabric that's back in fashion and easy to sew

by Connie Long

*i*t's impossible for me to resist purchasing beautiful pieces of lace, no matter how small. Just ⅛ yd. of a glorious, $300/yd. reembroidered or beaded lace provides several motifs to glamorize a neckline or shoulder, emphasize and dramatize a waist, or add distinction and spark to an evening jacket. Purchased appliqués look ordinary by comparison.

One of my favorite ways to use lace is in an entire garment, instead of just for trim. Lace separates—jacket (photo at left), tunic, or vest—are more versatile than a special occasion, one-piece garment that is destined to spend its life ever after in a closet. Lace changes dramatically depending on what is worn under or with it—a short metallic dress, evening pants, silk slip, or shorts.

For all its beautiful complexity, lace is not a finicky fabric. The author wears an Alençon lace jacket, completely underlined with polyester organza. You'd have to look very closely to see that the neck and front edges are appliquéd in place. (All photos except p. 49 by Susan Kahn)

Lace may look fragile and difficult to handle, but it is quite stable and forgiving of errors compared to other sheer fabrics. While it does require special attention to layout, lace has no grain, which means it can be cut in any appealing direction, and it does not fray. Minor mistakes often go unnoticed. After giving you some pointers on how to find quality lace, I'll share some techniques for layout and construction so you can give your own garments a couture finish.

Selecting an appropriate lace

Originally laces were painstakingly made by hand from finely spun linen. Fortunately, machines can now produce good-quality laces; many retain the name of the location where a similar type of lace was once handmade. (See "A guide to lace" at right.)

Most of the fanciest laces are imported. They are generally sold in narrow bolts, 30 in. to 36 in. wide, with prices that fall into three ranges. An unembellished lace starts at about $39/yd.; those with any metallic threads start at about $69/yd.; and laces with beads, sequins, metallic threads, and other embellishments range from $179/yd. to more than $300/yd. Edgings can cost anywhere from $2 to more than $100/yd.

A good lace has a varied surface and design interest with different textures, assorted motifs, and several net designs. Today laces are being made of cotton, rayon, nylon, silk, wool, metallic yarns, or linen. Most often they are a combination of several of these fibers.

Reembroidered laces, such as Alençon, and other novelty laces have motifs outlined in cords, ribbons, sequins, or yarns that are applied by hand-guided machines after the lace is made. Garments made with these most expensive laces are candidates for appliquéd seams. Laces with large sheer areas between motifs look best when sewn with small, neat seams.

Before you select a lace, analyze its design and think of the garment you want to make. Are the motifs balanced and do they have a specific direction? If both edges are scalloped, do they have the same motif? Do the edge motifs form a mirror image?

If the lace is sequinned, beaded, or ribboned, check the structure of the stitching on the back. Well-designed laces allow you to separate motifs with minimal bead or surface-design loss. Poorly designed laces often have a continuous beading thread; when motifs are cut apart, beads are lost. An exception is borders, which by design have a continuous thread.

If you are planning to sew beaded lace by

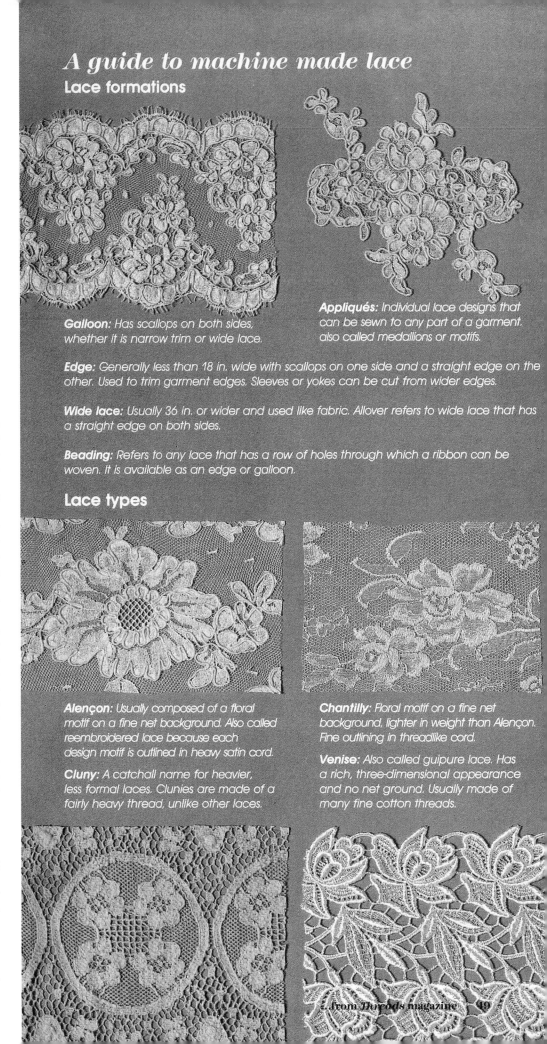

A guide to machine made lace
Lace formations

Galloon: Has scallops on both sides, whether it is narrow trim or wide lace.

Appliqués: Individual lace designs that can be sewn to any part of a garment, also called medallions or motifs.

Edge: Generally less than 18 in. wide with scallops on one side and a straight edge on the other. Used to trim garment edges. Sleeves or yokes can be cut from wider edges.

Wide lace: Usually 36 in. or wider and used like fabric. Allover refers to wide lace that has a straight edge on both sides.

Beading: Refers to any lace that has a row of holes through which a ribbon can be woven. It is available as an edge or galloon.

Lace types

Alençon: Usually composed of a floral motif on a fine net background. Also called reembroidered lace because each design motif is outlined in heavy satin cord.

Cluny: A catchall name for heavier, less formal laces. Clunies are made of a fairly heavy thread, unlike other laces.

Chantilly: Floral motif on a fine net background, lighter in weight than Alençon. Fine outlining in threadlike cord.

Venise: Also called guipure lace. Has a rich, three-dimensional appearance and no net ground. Usually made of many fine cotton threads.

All the lace edges of Connie Long's rayon-and-metallic-thread Chantilly lace and silk organza dress were appliquéd in place. The bodice also has two appliquéd darts.

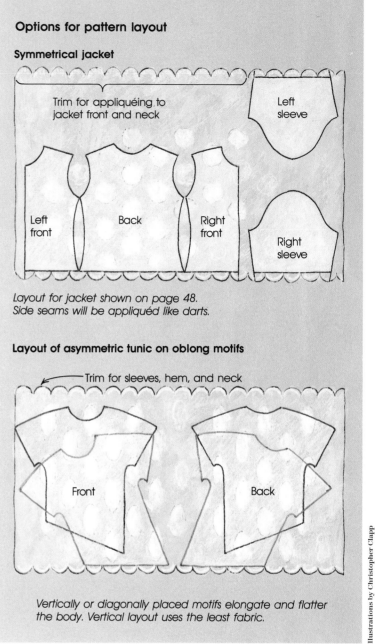

Options for pattern layout

Symmetrical jacket

Trim for appliquéing to jacket front and neck

Left sleeve

Left front

Back

Right front

Right sleeve

Layout for jacket shown on page 48. Side seams will be appliquéd like darts.

Layout of asymmetric tunic on oblong motifs

Trim for sleeves, hem, and neck

Front

Back

Vertically or diagonally placed motifs elongate and flatter the body. Vertical layout uses the least fabric.

machine, select one that has beads or pearls confined to motif centers so that you can sew around them; you can sew through sequins. If necessary, use a zipper foot for stitching close to a beaded area, but always test the stitch tension first.

If lace has beading or sequins, it's riskier to dry clean it than to hand wash it yourself. I like to hand wash lace garments, but I test the lace before I cut it. One rayon lace I used shrank considerably and became softer, but at least I didn't have to worry about what the dry cleaning solvents would do to the color of the beads I added.

If you *must* press sequinned lace, do so from the back using a low setting, a press cloth, and absolutely no steam. Lace that is pressed face down on terrycloth will retain its raised texture. If the seams are appliquéd, they lie flat and don't need pressing.

Layout takes longer than sewing

Beautiful lace works well as the focal point of a garment with a simple silhouette and minimal seams. Seams that interrupt motifs, design flow, and harmony detract from the finished garment.

I usually shop for lace with a garment design in mind, but I always remain flexible so that a specific lace can be taken into account. When selecting a commercial pattern, always zero in on the shape and seams rather than the frills and finishes, which can easily be changed or eliminated.

Once you've selected a pattern, make adjustments and a muslin, if necessary, to correct the fit. Duplicate the corrected pattern so that you have a full front and back plus both sleeves for layout. The corrected muslin can also be used as a pattern. Clearly mark the seamlines, center front, center

back, and darts. If the pattern gives cutting lines only, draw the seamlines, because they will be your points of reference. Finished hemlines should also be marked.

Bring the corrected pattern with you when you purchase the lace. Lace is so expensive that you'll want to check the yardage by laying out the pattern pieces on the lace, as shown in the drawing above. Even if a commercial pattern calls for lace, the layouts are too general and too traditional to apply to specific lace and there can be a considerable difference in the amount of fabric that is actually needed. A T-shaped tunic generally requires about 1½ yd.

You'll need to make sure that there is enough edging or scallops to finish all garment edges. If you're using white, ecru, or black lace, you can often purchase trim with complimentary motifs separately. How-

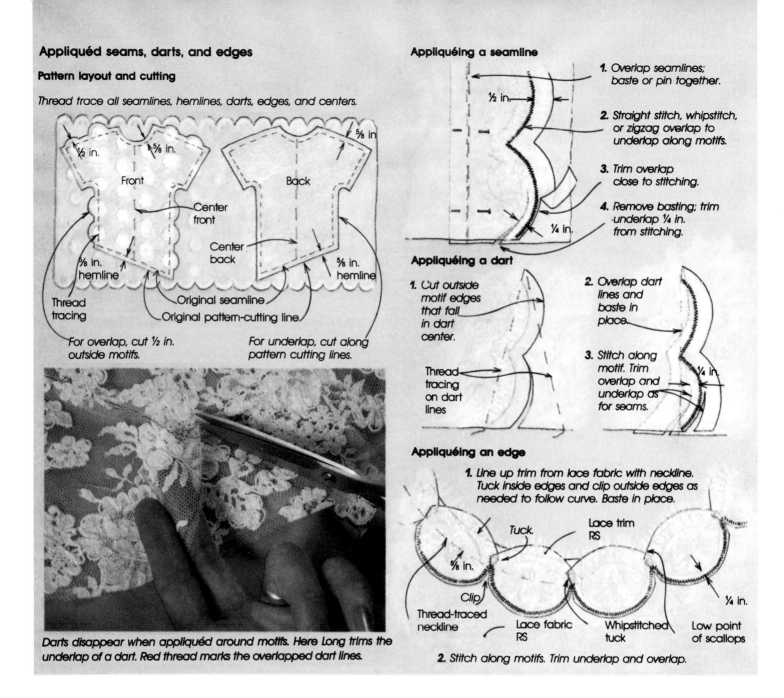

Appliquéd seams, darts, and edges

Pattern layout and cutting

Thread trace all seamlines, hemlines, darts, edges, and centers.

½ in.   ⅝ in.   ⅝ in

Front   Back

Center front

Center back

⅝ in. hemline

⅝ in. hemline

Thread tracing

Original seamline

Original pattern-cutting line

For overlap, cut ½ in. outside motifs.

For underlap, cut along pattern cutting lines.

Darts disappear when appliquéd around motifs. Here Long trims the underlap of a dart. Red thread marks the overlapped dart lines.

Appliquéing a seamline

½ in.

1. Overlap seamlines; baste or pin together.

2. Straight stitch, whipstitch, or zigzag overlap to underlap along motifs.

3. Trim overlap close to stitching.

4. Remove basting; trim underlap ¼ in. from stitching.

¼ in.

Appliquéing a dart

1. Cut outside motif edges that fall in dart center.

Thread tracing on dart lines

2. Overlap dart lines and baste in place.

3. Stitch along motif. Trim overlap and underlap as for seams.

¼ in.

Appliquéing an edge

1. Line up trim from lace fabric with neckline. Tuck inside edges and clip outside edges as needed to follow curve. Baste in place.

Tuck.

Lace trim RS

⅝ in.

Clip

Thread-traced neckline

Lace fabric RS

Whipstitched tuck

Low point of scallops

¼ in.

2. Stitch along motifs. Trim underlap and overlap.

---

ever, when using a novelty lace with metallic embroidery, ribbons, cords, multicolors, or beading, the scalloped trim must come from the main fabric.

During the layout, place the lace on a table of contrasting color or on a fabric ground so that the motifs are prominent. Explore pattern placement possibilities, and position the pieces according to the appearance of lace motifs within the pattern shape. If the pattern is opaque, slip it *under* the lace. The most important considerations are motif placement, balance, and overall attractive appearance.

Usually I prefer to cut a garment so that the scalloped lace edges line up with as many finished garment edges as is most economical. Laces often have directional designs. Position prominent motifs so that they are flattering to the body, as shown for oblong motifs in the lower drawing and

photo on the facing page.

When I've brought the fabric home, I like to pin the pattern to the lace with fine glass-head pins; regular heads tend to go right through the lace. I like to mark first and then cut. Use contrasting colorfast thread to trace all seamlines, hems (except for those placed along scallops), necklines, center front and back, darts, and any useful construction marks. You can use disappearing markers, but always test them first. Thread tracing is quicker and easier than it sounds; flip the layout so that the lace is on top and the pattern, still pinned, is on the bottom. Since laces are fairly transparent you can still see the pattern sewing lines. Baste only through the lace.

Hidden seams

Appliquéd seams are invisible when well

done, and they are effective for reembroidered laces with small sheer areas, such as Alençon, Chantilly, and Venise. The seams are overlapped and the top layer is stitched to the underlap following the edges of motifs; the process sequence for seams, darts, and edges are shown in the drawings above.

For the tunic shown in the upper left drawing, I cut the front shoulders and side seams around motif edges. Trim from the fabric was appliquéd to the neckline and hems. Don't worry if the motifs from the front don't match the placement of motifs in the back; most of the underlap will be trimmed. Cut the tunic back (underlap) with ⅝-in. seam allowances.

When there is enough lace, I cut both the front and the back around motifs. I can remove the motifs from the underlap and use them for another project.

Overlap the thread-traced seamlines and pin or baste (drawing at top right, previous page). Also pin or baste along the motif edges of the overlap. Stitch the overlap to the underlap along the motif edges; I use a machine straight stitch and have not had any problems. Always test the stitch on scraps first. If your machine has a large needle hole in its plate, cover the entire hole with clear tape; the needle will make its own smaller opening. Lace may be dragged down into a large hole. If the feed dogs abrade the lace, place crisp tracing paper under the lace for protection and support. Then trim the overlap close to the stitching. Trim the underlap to ¼-in. (photo on p. 51).

Darts can also be appliquéd. For best results, position the pattern during layout so that motif edges fall within the dart (drawing at center right, p. 51). Clip around the motif edges that fall in the dart center. Overlap the stitching lines and baste in place. Stitch following motif edges and trim.

Garment edges can be finished with separate motifs (lower right drawing, p. 51). Cut the fabric border along the motifs and save it for garment trim.

For a curved edge like a neckline, you'll have to clip the lace trim on the outside curve and tuck it on the inside curve so that it lies flat. To position trim on a neckline, place the garment on a dress form. Place the lace so that the low points of the trim scallops coincide with the thread-traced neckline. Baste the scalloped outside edge to the neck edge by hand or machine, and then stitch following motif curves. Hand sew tiny tucks between scallops with a whipstitch. Trim the underlap to ¼ in., following curves carefully.

Repeat the process for garment and sleeve hems. Clipping and tucking are required only for curved edges.

Facings and finishing

A scalloped facing supports a neckline that could become floppy or stretched. Silk, polyester, or nylon organza or chiffon is an excellent choice for facings or for a crisp, sheer lining.

The best color choice is either a subdued version of the lace's background color or one that matches your skin tone. Do a hand test first. Place the organza over the back of your hand, and then put the lace over the organza to cover both your hand and your bare arm. Choose the color that blends best with the tone of your bare skin or that shows no line of demarcation. Usually a tone darker than your skin looks more natural. Too light a color can look fleshy and prominent. Aim for the sheerest and least-obvious tone.

The sequence of facing layout and stitching is shown in the drawing below. Cut enlarged front and back facings. Sew the facing pieces together and then trim and press the seam allowances.

With wrong sides together, position the facing inside the neckline, matching the shoulder seamlines. The facing neckline edges should extend past the scalloped neckline edges of the lace. Pin or baste in place. With white dressmaker's carbon and a tracing wheel, trace the scalloped neckline edge onto the sheer facing.

Remove the facing from the garment. Staystitch the traced scallop line of the facing, making sure to pivot neatly where scallops meet. Trim the seam allowance outside the staystitching and clip to the stitching between the scallops.

Position the facing inside the garment again (photo below). Fold the facing's seam allowances toward the garment along the stitching and slipstitch in place. Trim the facing's lower edge to match the motif contours and slipstitch in place.

You can use shoulder pads in a lace garment to square the silhouette. Although they will show somewhat, they cushion the garment's shoulder area and remove some stress from the seams. Use the same criteria to select an organza color for the shoulder pads as you did for the facing, or buy a pair whose color blends well. The alternative is to dye a pair using tea, coffee, or Rit dye. Always test dip a tiny corner first. Remember that the pads should be inconspicuous, just like the facing. □

Connie Long, who teaches classes on sewing specialty fabrics at G Street Fabrics in Rockville, MD, is a free-lance clothing designer in Mitchellville, MD.

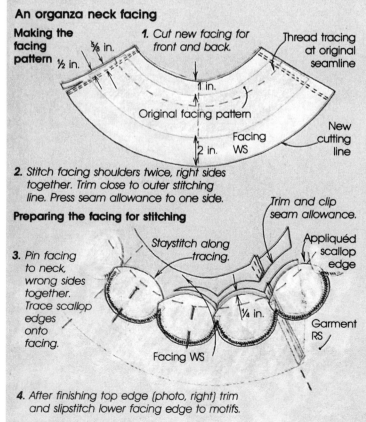

An organza neck facing

Making the facing pattern ½ in. ⅝ in.

1. Cut new facing for front and back.

Thread tracing at original seamline

1 in.

Original facing pattern

Facing WS

New cutting line

2 in.

2. Stitch facing shoulders twice, right sides together. Trim close to outer stitching line. Press seam allowance to one side.

Preparing the facing for stitching

3. Pin facing to neck, wrong sides together. Trace scallop edges onto facing.

Staystitch along tracing.

Trim and clip seam allowance.

Appliquéd scallop edge

¼ in.

Garment RS

Facing WS

4. After finishing top edge (photo, right) trim and slipstitch lower facing edge to motifs.

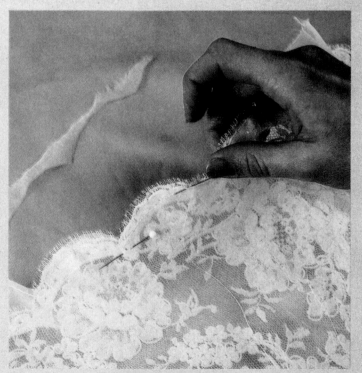

The sheer organza facing has been staystitched and trimmed to shape. Long folds the edge under and slipstitches it to the lace edge, wrong sides together.

Couture Quilting

Geoffrey Beene adds structure and decoration to both day and evening wear with channel stitching

by Roberta Carr

If there was a "couture" in the United States, Geoffrey Beene would be my choice for the leading couturier. He can give weightless fabric volume and structure without weighing it down, effortlessly transform a garment with the simplest of details, and combine the perfect garments into totally unified and inspired outfits, like the one described in "A walk through a Geoffrey Beene original" on p. 56. I've studied his miraculous results for years. Yet of all the techniques that his creations have inspired me to explore, the one that's been the most useful to me is a machine-quilting technique known as channel stitching.

With carefully chosen and precisely positioned rows of parallel machine stitching, Beene adds stiffness and body to soft fabrics, uses that structure to enhance the figure, and adds pattern to plain color and texture to flat fabric. Channel stitching is similar to quilting or decorative topstitching, although those are much broader categories; Geoffrey Beene calls it "liquid geometry." What I refer to as channel stitching is at least three parallel (or nearly so) lines of topstitching grouped together on a garment for decorative effect. Because the more lines of stitching you add to a piece or layers of fabric, the more you stiffen it, channel stitching usually has some structural function as well, and it can incorporate construction stitching, too. Whatever you call it, it's a technique that any home sewer can take advantage of.

Channel stitching has many components, and there are an infinite number of ways to put them together, but in its simplest form, you can add channel stitching to any garment with nothing more than the thread and interfacing you're already using. Let's look at how to add simple, straight rows of channel stitching at the easiest and most likely places, the cuff and the hem, and then examine its more varied uses in the hands of a master like Beene.

Channel-stitched cuffs

Cuffs are a good place to start exploring channel stitching because the stiffening effect is usually just what you want, and not much can go wrong. The area to stitch is small, so the multiple rows go quickly. You could try this out on either a two-piece or a folded-over cuff. I use only natural-fiber fabrics, because of their responsiveness to the techniques of couture sewing—in other words, techniques which are more concerned with perfection than with speed. Simple though the idea of channel stitching is, the care required for perfect results can be considerable, so it's definitely a couture, and not a ready-to-wear, technique. Still, cuffs are easy.

Unlike channel stitching in other areas (which is often done on finished garment sections, stitching across seams if necessary), that for cuffs is done before they're constructed. I apply interfacing to the wrong side of the outer part of the cuff only, not to the part that will be against the wrist. I would most likely choose a fusible, perhaps an all-bias like Sof-shape, or a woven or weft insertion like Armo Wisper Weft, cut on the bias. For a lightweight silk such as crepe de chine, I'd choose Silk-Weight, an ultra-thin woven fusible, and cut it on the bias. The flexibility of a bias-cut interfacing won't interfere with the smooth curve of the cuff when it's worn.

It's important not to add any unnecessary bulk to the seams, so the interfacing must not extend into the seam allowances. Cut it the length of the cuff only, so the ends will tuck under the allowances after they're folded back. Start and stop each row of stitches just past the seamlines so the allowances aren't stiffened. You don't want to make lots of little knots, so begin and end with a few stitches at a near-zero stitch length, and clip the threads close. Channel stitching dulls needles quickly, so start with a new one, and change them frequently. To mark seamlines, thread trace them with silk thread so you can see them from either side.

Perfectly smooth, distortion-free channel stitching depends on the proper sequence of stitching and pressing. In order to make absolutely sure that the stitching doesn't gradually throw the piece you're stitching off grain, you must straighten and press the entire piece after each row is stitched.

Always press lightly from the right side of the fabric with an appropriate press cloth and light moisture if necessary, depending on the fabric. Press with the iron held perpendicular to the rows of stitching, moving sideways and overlapping the pressed areas. When all the rows have been stitched, finish the cuffs as usual.

Preparing for hems

Hems are also an ideal place for channel stitching. The stitches stabilize and add weight to the hem, and the multiple layers of fabric enhance the stitching. With pale, transparent fabrics, a channel-stitched hem can convert the unattractive show-through of a plain hem facing into an attention-getting virtue. Hems of skirts, pants, jackets, coats, and sleeves can all be treated in the same way, and these techniques will apply to faced necklines as well. But before you plunge into the various techniques I'll describe for different hem treatments, you've got to make some decisions.

Options—Typically, all you want to do at the hem is enhance a design you've already settled on. But because hems are so

Beene loves to appliqué glossy, freeform shapes to plainer fabrics with concentric rows of channel stitching.

much larger than cuffs, and are an integral part of the main garment pieces, it's important to think carefully about the effect you want the channel stitching to achieve. If you make the hem too stiff or heavy, you could spoil the garment. With cuffs, you're probably safe adding a few rows of stitching just before you attach them, but for hems, you ought to know exactly how you plan to channel stitch the garment before you even cut it out.

Among the choices you need to make for even the simplest channel-stitched hem are: How many rows of stitching? How far apart? And what size should the stitches be? The degree of stiffening you get from channel stitching is determined by all of these things, in combination with your inner and outer fabric choices. And what about interfacing, or batting, or no filling at all? The visibility of your stitching depends on the thickness and softness of the layers.

I am often asked how designers get the perfect results they so often achieve. The answer is testing. Every effortless, faultless creation is a final result, the cumulative solution to the dozens of problems encountered in search of just the right fabric, the right interfacing, and the perfect technique. If we want to approach their results with our own sewing, we have to do the same thing, as well as we can with our resources. I suggest you buy at least an additional ¼ yd. of the fashion fabric for testing for any garment you plan to put couture effort into.

Testing—Length of stitch in relation to a specific thread type can be varied to create many different effects. To determine which is best for your design, layer a 1-in. by 20-in. piece of fabric with the interfacing or batting you think you'd like to use (discussed at more length below). Start at 6 st. per inch and stitch for 2 in., change to 8 st., then progress to 10, 12, 16, 18, 20, etc. so that you have at least 2 in. of stitching for each stitch length. Look at your result up close, then look at it from 3 ft. away as someone would see it if they were standing next to you. Notice how denser stitching makes the fabric stiffer. Mark your preferred length and keep the sample with a tag identifying the fabric and thread you used.

To test the width between rows, use a 6-in. by 6-in. sample of fabric with your chosen (or possible) backing. Select three options, for example, ⅜ in. apart, ½ in. apart, and ⅝ in. apart, then stitch about 2 in. of each width. Notice how closer rows of stitching make the sample stiffer.

By now you should know whether your interfacing choice will work, and hopefully you'll be done testing, or will have to test only one width or length on another backing. Unfortunately, the only way to know for certain that your final choices are appropriate is to make a garment with them. In fact, each garment you make is a test, and that's how you develop experience. If you start with channel-stitched hems and cuffs, and perhaps a neckline, you'll soon feel confident.

Choosing hem interfacing

An interfaced hem is actually a series of concentric circles: garment, interfacing, and hem. Each inner circle needs to be smaller than the one outside it in order for the hem to remain undistorted. How much smaller depends on the thickness of the fabric and the interfacing. Since the interfacing can't extend into the seam allowances, you'll cut separate pieces for each skirt section. Cut them so they're a little narrower than the section they interface.

Unless your side seams are perfectly vertical, the hem will be bigger than the garment, and it needs to be shrunk to fit inside. You can do this with heat and steam on all natural fibers—and most easily on wool—after you turn the hem. But to preserve the shaping after you start channel stitching, it's important always to press from the right side of the garment and to work over a shaped surface like a tailors' ham or a seam roll.

Sew-in interfacing—As with cuffs, hems should be interfaced with bias-cut interfacing, whether sewn in or fused. Silk organza, Dura-Press, and tailors' hair canvas are all "user-friendly" choices (listed in order of increasing weight), depending on the weight of the outer fabric, if you don't want a puffy, quilted effect.

Start by thread tracing the hemline with silk thread so it can be seen from both sides of the garment. All the vertical seams should already be complete. Cut

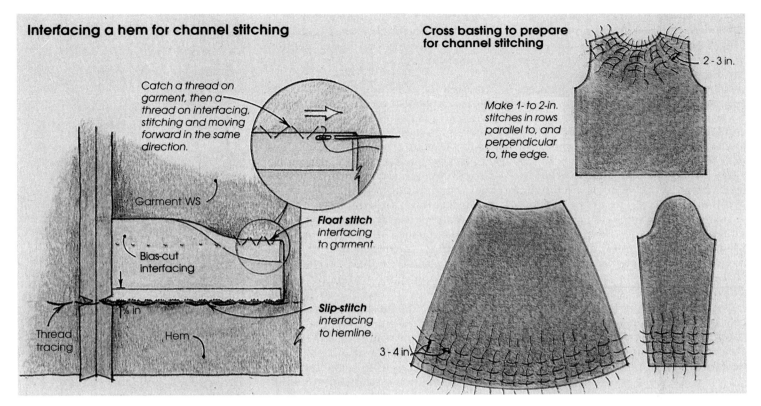

Interfacing a hem for channel stitching

Catch a thread on garment, then a thread on interfacing, stitching and moving forward in the same direction.

Garment WS

Bias-cut interfacing

Thread tracing

⅝ in

Hem

Float stitch interfacing to garment.

Slip-stitch interfacing to hemline.

Cross basting to prepare for channel stitching

2 - 3 in.

Make 1- to 2-in. stitches in rows parallel to, and perpendicular to, the edge.

3 - 4 in.

the interfacing on the bias the length between the vertical seams and the width of the finished hem plus 1¼ in. Lay the interfacing on the wrong side of the garment so that it overlaps the marked hemline by ⅝ in., as shown in the left-hand drawing above. The extra layer of interfacing helps to keep the hem edge soft. Pin it in place from the right side of the garment to ensure that the concentric-circle shaping is preserved, with no excess interfacing.

Working from the wrong side, lift up the overlapping ⅝ in. and slip-stitch it to the marked hemline. Then turn up the hem and pin it in place, again pinning from the right side.

To attach the interfacing to the garment, I use a float stitch (so called because two pieces of fabric attached with it float against each other); it's shown in the left-hand drawing above. I fold back the top edge of the interfacing and stitch one row (unless the hem is bias cut—then I'd stitch a few rows) about 1 in. down from the edge. Finish the hem edge as you choose, then float stitch the hem edge to the interfacing. Because this interfacing will be visible ⅝ in. above the hem on the inside, the hem will never be visible on the outside.

Fusible interfacing and batting—Refer to the cuff instructions for the brands of fusibles that I prefer to use. These should be cut the same way as just described, so that they overlap the hemline, don't

cross any seams, and the ends tuck under the seam allowances.

Most quilters' battings—no matter how thin—are designed for home decorating and are completely out of place in a couture garment. Thermore batting, available in many quilting and fabric shops, or by mail from The Fabric Carr, P.O. Box 32120, San Jose, CA 98152, (408) 929-1651, is designed specifically for garments. It's thin enough to be used in a hem between two layers of silk crepe de chine, and can even go into sleeves without making them too bulky. It's perfect for channel stitching.

Cut strips of batting the same size as the interfacing, except for the overlap at the hemline. The batting should just touch the marked hem and should be basted in place prior to turning up the hem.

Basting and stitching

No matter what interfacing or batting you've chosen, even none at all, the procedure for channel stitching hems (and other layered sections) is the same. When multiple rows of stitches are sewn in the same direction over layers of fabric, the underlayers tend to slip, distorting the grain. With each subsequent row of stitching, the slippage will increase. To prevent this, layers need to be basted by hand. It's very important to use silk thread for basting, because it will not make marks on the fabric, even under repeated pressing. And it's easy to remove when the machine stitching is complete.

To eliminate fabric movement in all directions, I use a technique called cross basting. To cross baste, take 1- to 2-in. stitches in rows perpendicular to the hem edge of the garment, as shown in the right-hand drawing above. The rows should be 3 to 4 in. apart at hems, and 2 to 3 in. apart at necklines. Next, hand baste with similar stitches parallel to the hem or neckline edge, with stitches spaced 1 to 2 in. apart.

To channel stitch, stitch one row at a distance from the hem equal to the predetermined width between rows, beginning at the hem edge and working on the right side of the garment. Start on the left back (not on a seam, so that you don't have to start over the extra bulk) at the planned stitch length.

Leave 3-in. tails on the thread so that after each row is pressed, you can pull the threads to the wrong side and tie them off. After all rows have been stitched and pressed, any excess hem allowance beyond the last row of stitches can simply be trimmed away, without adding any extra bulk. All the silk basting threads can now be removed.

Channel stitching a la Beene

Geoffrey Beene is a master at choosing just the right stitch length, thread, and design to bring fabric alive with channel stitching. No fabric seems to be inappropriate. He channel stitches on gabardine, silk crepe de chine, cotton, wool jersey, and silk satin. Besides hems and cuffs, he likes to channel stitch collars, yokes, shoulders, and necklines, on top of contrast fabrics that have been appliquéd onto his garments, and even all over entire garments, as on the bolero jacket in the photo at far right on the facing page. To achieve the weightless look for which he is renowned, Beene has layered a crepe-de-chine jacket or bodice that looks as if it has no structure at all, over a completely channel stitched lining that provides the needed shaping. Let's take a look at how to add channel stitching in some of these areas.

Yokes—A yoke can be channel stitched prior to sewing it to other parts of the garment. Cross baste interfacing or batting to the wrong side of the top yoke. To avoid unnecessary bulk, don't include interfacing or batting in any seam allowances, except to cover a shoulder seam. Channel stitch typically following the outline of the yoke itself, working from the outside edge into the neck edge.

Shoulders—Raglan sleeves can be particularly attractive with channel-stitched shoulders. If you add layers of interfacing and/or batting, these can substitute for shoulder pads. Cut interfacing or batting the length you want down the center of the sleeve from the neck edge, and wide enough to go out to each sleeve seam. Don't include it in any seam allowances, and cross baste as usual.

The rows of stitching could be straight and perpendicular to the armscye, creating a V design on the center line of the sleeve, or curved to follow the curve of the neckline.

Whole-garment channel stitching—There are two ways to channel stitch entire garments: either before cutting out the pattern shapes or after some of the seams are complete. The advantage of the first method is that the stitching is more straightforward. You don't have to work around any details or over any humps, and, since adding lots of stitches can slightly shrink the fabric, by cutting out the pattern pieces afterwards, they'll be more accurate. Cut out and stitch sections of fabric slightly larger than each pattern piece, rather than trying to channel stitch yardage.

The advantage to stitching over seams is that you don't have to match the channel-stitched rows. You'll want the garment as flat as possible, so choose a few prominent seams to finish first, like center front and shoulder seams, and leave the less-visible seams to do afterwards.

In either case, cross baste the entire sec-

tion as described above for small areas. If you're stitching on the bias, do each row in the same direction, then straighten the grain and press.

Appliqués—Beene loves contrast—glossy fabrics appliquéd and channel stitched onto dark, solid-colored garments—and he reserves these combinations for the most dramatic evening wear. He's stitched over waves, zigzags, concentric circles, spirals, and freeform swirls, as shown in the drawing on p. 54. A simple way to form and finish the edges of an appliquéd shape is to lay a piece of organza over the appliqué right sides together, with grains matching. Stitch the layers together along the outline you want. Cut into the center of the organza, and trim it away except for a ½- to 1-in. strip inside the stitching. Then fold the organza strip to the wrong side, and press the fold. If you so desire, you could insert batting or interfacing inside the strip. To keep the channel stitching from making the appliquéd section too stiff, you can stitch every other row on the appliqué alone, and then do the in-between rows through both the appliqué and the garment once the appliqué is in place.

Decorative threads—Beene is fond of contrast stitching, especially with gold thread, over his smooth, shiny appliquéd fabrics. We've got a wonderful range of thread types to pick from these days, in a huge number of colors. Do you want a quiet cotton, glossy rayon, or a glittering metallic? Silk can be delicate sewing thread or thick buttonhole twist. The color can be a high contrast to your fabric, a subtle shade darker or lighter, or a perfect match. Don't be afraid to use two different colors in alternating rows, or a variegated thread.

Topstitching needles have larger holes than regular needles of the same size and can help prevent skipped stitches with thick or textured decorative threads. I use an all-cotton thread in the bobbin with most topstitching threads, matching the background color so the stitches are distinct.

If you're getting lots of skipped stitches, stop and change something (needle, thread, tension . . .) until they go away. To fix isolated instances, complete the row, then catch the long stitch in the middle with a tiny hand stitch and tie off in the back of the work, so it looks exactly like all the other stitches—perfect. □

Roberta Carr is the author of Couture—The Fine Art of Sewing, *published by Palmer/Pletsch in 1992.*

A walk through a Geoffrey Beene original

by David Page Coffin

The first thing you notice about this Geoffrey Beene outfit from 1982 isn't the allover channel stitching on the jacket. Instead you see its effect: the soft structure of the bolero jacket that looks almost padded. In fact, the jacket is made of nothing but two fabrics channel stitched together. On the outside is the lightweight wool Beene used in the outfit's blouse. Inside, where the stitching is more obvious (top left photo on facing page), is an incredibly rich, heavy, napped alpaca in charcoal brown.

The channel stitching doesn't precisely match across the binding-covered seams, so each section was evidently done separately. The binding strips, cut from the same ultra-fine wool jersey as the skirt, cover the seams inside and out, and there's absolutely no bulk underneath. To duplicate this, you could bind the seams from the right side after stitching them, then completely trim away the seam allowances or even the seam itself, since the binding will be holding everything secure. The second binding should be slightly wider than the first, so that its edge stitching falls just outside the binding on the other side.

Shaping each side below the sleeve seam is a dart tapering from nothing at the hem to about ¾ in. in the middle, and back to nothing at the sleeve. It's not cut open or trimmed, but pressed to the back and hand stitched down. At the hem edge in back are two covered weights, to keep the jacket from riding forward.

The skirt is channel stitched at the hem with nine rows of ⅜-in.-spaced stitches. After a ¾-in. gap, there's a 1-in.-wide channel at the top that's been lightly stuffed with a soft filler, creating a slightly raised effect. The hem section has been interfaced with a fusible of some kind. There's no channel stitching on the blouse, but the stuffed collars and cuffs (lower photo) repeat the padded theme.

Channel stitching at its everyday best: *This Beene ensemble from 1982 (right) gets its shape from a jacket of channel-stitch-joined layers and a channel-stitched hem. On the inside, above, the jacket reveals its allover channel stitching and its alpaca un-derlayer. All seams are bound in strips of the skirt material. The skirt hem is channel stitched and padded in the top row only.*

The bib-front blouse (directly above) is made from the same lightweight wool fabric as the outer jacket layer, and its neckline and cuffs are outlined in heavy covered cord.

Embellishing with Fabric

Trims adapted from the nineteenth century decorate clothing in the twentieth

by Adrienne Saint-Pierre

*f*or years I've been fascinated by the elaborate fabric and ribbon trims so prevalent on nineteenth-century women's clothing. Dressmakers of the day often devised their own techniques, and as the century went on, the trims became fancier and fancier. When I spot one on a garment in a museum collection or on the rack of an antique clothing store, I always try to figure out how it was constructed. Then I go home and try to duplicate the trim. Shown here and on pp. 60-61 are only a few of the trims that I've encountered.

Once you've tried the technique, you'll probably think of several ways to use it, such as on women's and children's clothing, bridal and prom gowns, or on fashion or home accessories.

You may even invent a few variations! Further inspiration is easy to come by if you study some of the elaborate gowns—or even the simple yet finely sewn examples—made in the last century. Let's see if we can recover the lost art of dressmakers' trims. ⇨

Adrienne Saint-Pierre of Redding, CT, has worked as a costume curator for historical societies. Currently, she teaches workshops on vintage sewing techniques and reproduces 19th-century wedding gowns.

(For more on vintage trims, see the article on making ribbon flowers in Threads No. 44, pp. 40-44, *and the article on folded and gathered ribbon trims in* Threads No. 12, pp. 58-63. *The latter is reprinted in the book* Stitchery and Needle Lace *(Taunton Press, 1991).*

An elegant silk trim adapted from the train of an 1880s wedding gown looks beautiful on the lapel of a modern dress (based on now-out-of-print Vogue 7773). It's made by pleating and folding a bias ruffle to form pockets that resemble a row of lush flowers.

It only takes 7 folds of fabric and 28 stitches sawteeth to complete a holiday ornament, sewn from a vintage linen dinner napkin. After clipping the fold at even intervals, you poke the sides of each tab inward to make triangles, then overcast.

Constructing sawtooth edging

A hand-sewing technique that both finishes and decorates a straight-grain fold, sawtooth edging was often stitched around the hems and ruffles of 19th-century petticoats and nightgowns. Sewn on tightly woven linen or cotton, the trim looks delicate but makes a sturdy finish. Try sawtooth edging on the collar, cuffs, tucks, or placket of a crisp white blouse.

Extra-fine sewing thread (such as Coats & Clark Extra-Fine Dual Duty) and a fine needle (such as a No. 10 milliners' needle) help to make the stitches invisible. You'll need sewing or embroidery scissors with a sharp point, and a see-through grid ruler makes marking easier.

Equilateral triangles give the trim a pleasing look. To achieve this effect, the depth of the clips must be slightly shorter than the distance between clips (e.g., ⅜ in. wide and ⁵⁄₁₆ in. deep). When poking the tabs inward to make points, stroke the point of the needle down inside the fold, pushing the fabric all the way to the bottom of the clip. I usually find it easiest to push in too much fabric, then use the needle point to gently pull back on the fold until it is centered on the tab. —A.S.

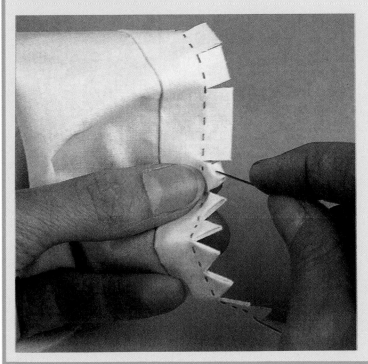

Start by folding fabric and pressing crease sharply.

1 **Mark and cut**—Mark even triangle widths along fold with pins or sharp pencil. Hand baste with thread to mark depth, then clip as marked.

2 **Fold points**—Push right half of tab to inside with tip of needle. Crease with forefinger and thumbnail. Repeat stroking and creasing on left side of tab.

3 **Stitch**—Using tiny overcast stitches, sew along sides of triangle, securing bottom of clip with two stitches.

From *Threads* magazine (December 1993) 50:66-69

Making the magical row of bows

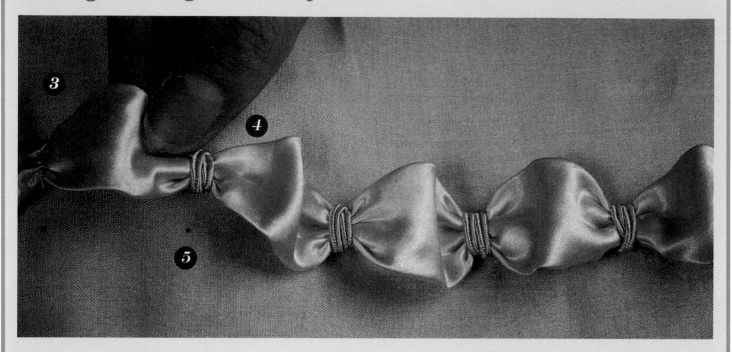

Although a row of bows appears difficult to make, it is actually easy, and is by far the favorite of my workshop students. The technique is comparable to an ingenious magic trick, as it is lovely, yet simple. Use a soft, medium-weight fabric, such as satin, for the bows, a narrow braid for the wraps, and a firm backing fabric, such as silk pongee or moiré.

I've seen the row of bows on an antique garment only once, edging the wide, low neckline of a violet silk bodice from the 1860s, with the trim in ivory satin. You can use this trim in many ways, such as around the waistband of a little girl's dress, or on accessories from bridal headpieces and barrettes to evening bags. I placed it between the full double sleeve puffs on an 1860s-style wedding gown.

A few sewing hints: When adding braid to the gathered strip, a slightly crossed wrap looks attractive. Don't wrap the braid too tightly or the bows will look strangled. To shape the bows with the tip of an iron, fold and lightly flatten the excess fabric, creating the illusion of soft, overlapping bows. —A.S.

1. *Bows are made by folding and tacking down a soft bias tube of fabric. Cut a 2½-in.-wide bias strip, press one long raw edge under, fold long edge to center back 1⅛ in. wide, and press.*

2. *Mark bias strip at 1¾-in. intervals and backing fabric at 1¼-in. intervals.*

3. ***Gather***—*At mark on bias, handsew across strip and back. Pull up; secure but do not cut thread.*

4. ***Wrap***—*Sew end of braid to center back, wrap twice, and anchor at back with thread. Cut braid but not thread.*

5. ***Tack down***—*Sew wrap to mark on fabric, creating a puff between wraps. Cut thread. Complete steps 3-5 at each mark.*

6. ***Puffs form bows***—*Gently fold and press puffs in alternating directions. Tack lower two layers of corners to backing fabric.*

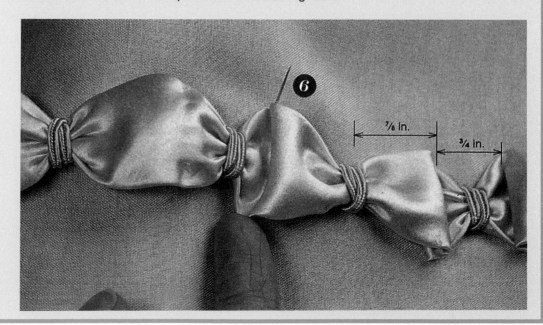

⅞ in.

¾ in.

Creating petal pockets

The elegant flowers shown on p. 58 are made by pleating and folding a ruffle to form pockets, with bias loops sewn inside to represent stamens.

Use lustrous fabric with body, such as satin or taffeta, for the flowers. You'll need a 5-in.-wide bias strip about 2½ times the desired finished length of the trim, plus extra fabric for the stamens. For the base fabric, choose a fabric with body to disguise the thick seams, and interface the top layer.

First decide which way the flowers will open. On my dress, the flowers open upward; for a circular collar, you could change the direction of the pleats at the center back, so all the flowers open upwards. When you sew the ruffle to the base fabric, baste right sides together with the pleats facing in the direction that the flowers will open. Baste the facing to the other side of the ruffle and stitch a ½-in. seam. Understitch, then trim the seam allowance in layers.

It can be tricky to finish the trim ends neatly. At the top edge of my lapel, I curved the end to resemble a complete flower and stitched the raw edge into the seam. At the bottom, I folded the trim under and sewed the raw edge into the seam, where I graded the seam allowance carefully to avoid a lumpy spot. —A.S.

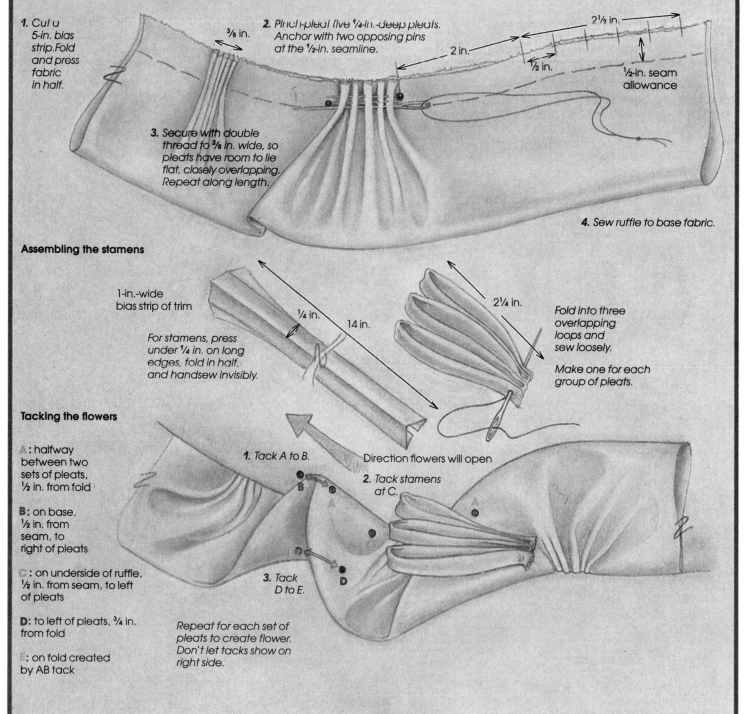

1. Cut a 5-in. bias strip. Fold and press fabric in half.

2. Pinch-pleat five ¼-in.-deep pleats. Anchor with two opposing pins at the ½-in. seamline.

⅜ in.

2 in.

2½ in.

½ in.

½-in. seam allowance

3. Secure with double thread to ⅜ in. wide, so pleats have room to lie flat, closely overlapping. Repeat along length.

4. Sew ruffle to base fabric.

Assembling the stamens

1-in.-wide bias strip of trim

¼ in.

14 in.

2¼ in.

For stamens, press under ¼ in. on long edges, fold in half, and handsew invisibly.

Fold into three overlapping loops and sew loosely.

Make one for each group of pleats.

Tacking the flowers

A: halfway between two sets of pleats, ½ in. from fold

B: on base, ½ in. from seam, to right of pleats

C: on underside of ruffle, ½ in. from seam, to left of pleats

D: to left of pleats, ¾ in. from fold

E: on fold created by AB tack

1. Tack A to B.

Direction flowers will open

2. Tack stamens at C.

3. Tack D to E.

Repeat for each set of pleats to create flower. Don't let tacks show on right side.

Dior Roses
Add a touch of haute couture

by Roberta Carr

a couture touch, a designer detail, a signature: designers since the dawn of haute couture have made flowers and trims from ribbons and fabric, but none is as famous as the Dior rose. Dior allowed his roses to cascade down ball-gown backs; he used them to call attention to the nipped waists on suit jackets and evening dresses. The roses are made from football-shaped fabric petals which are cut and folded on the bias, then gathered and stitched together. The variations within this framework are endless.

Making the Dior rose

You can easily duplicate the elegance of Dior's rose at home, using organdy, satin, taffeta, or any fabric which harmonizes with your project. Begin by cutting football shapes from the fabric in small, medium, and large sizes. Suggested dimensions are shown in the top left drawing, facing page.

Cut each petal so that the line running the length of the football is on the true bias. This will give a soft edge to each petal and at the same time prevent the finished rose from crushing, since bias doesn't wrinkle.

Begin with a small shape. Fold it lengthwise on the bias line, and run one or two rows of machine gathering stitches ¼ inch from the raw edge. Take two small stitches with a threaded needle in the gathering allowance at one end, as shown at top right, facing page. Leaving this needle hanging, begin to gather up the stitches and gently roll the gathered edge, as shown in the center photograph on the facing page. When it becomes difficult to hold the rolled petal and continue gathering, take a few hand stitches to hold the rolled petal in place. Do not tie off the thread at the end of the petal.

A profusion of roses graces a gown in the tradition of Dior. (Fashion illustration by Jacques Alschech)

From *Threads* magazine (April 1991) 34:72-73

As you gather up a medium shape, wrap it around the small rolled center and tack the two petals together as needed. Add a large shape, then tie off the thread.

I make three of these petal groups and hand overcast them together from the wrong side to duplicate the look of Dior's rose. You may like yours with only one or two groups, or you may want to add larger petals around the outside of the three-petal groupings.

If you are making one removable flower for a suit jacket or lapel, cover the base. Cut two circles the size of the base plus a ¼-in. seam allowance. Machine stitch, leaving 1 in. open to turn, and trim the seam to ⅛ in. Turn and press. Whipstitch the circle to the bottom of the flower using small stitches.

If you are applying flowers to a garment permanently, you don't need to cover the base of each flower, because it will be hidden when the flowers are whipstitched to the garment itself.

Variations

Now the fun begins! Once you have mastered the technique of making a Dior rose, you can make some small, some very large. A taffeta rose will look very different from an organza rose of the same size. Several fabrics can be used in the same flower. Alternate taffeta and organza—or taffeta, satin, and organza.

To get a hint of color in the center of the flower, you can cut the smallest football in two pieces and seam on what was the fold. Be sure the stitching line is on the true bias and stretch as you sew. Press the seam, first open, then closed. Trim the seam allowance back to a scant ⅛ in. You can then gather the raw edges and create petals as described above. This hint of color gives dimension to the flower while picking up colors that may appear in other parts of the garment.

To make a different style of rose, use one long continuous piece of bias. Mark a bias line on the fashion fabric. Using the bias line as the center, draw a necktie-shaped strip 20 in. long and 5 in. wide at one end, tapering to 2 in.

Fold on the center line and run two rows of machine gathering stitches along the raw edges. Hang a needle and thread from the small end as you do for the Dior rose, and begin pulling up gathers and rolling at the same time. Use the needle to tack the layers together whenever the rose becomes unmanageable. Again, these can be made as small or as large as desired by varying the length and width of your bias strip. □

Roberta Carr is owner of The Fabric Carr, a design studio and sewing school in San Jose, CA. A sewing tool catalog and class information is available from The Fabric Carr, PO Box 32120, San Jose, CA 95152; (408) 929-1651.

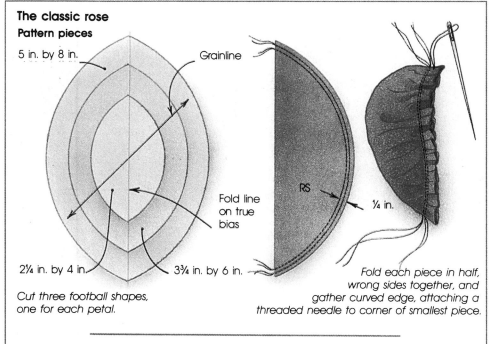

The classic rose
Pattern pieces

5 in. by 8 in.

Grainline

Fold line on true bias

RS

¼ in.

2¼ in. by 4 in.

3¾ in. by 6 in.

Cut three football shapes, one for each petal.

Fold each piece in half, wrong sides together, and gather curved edge, attaching a threaded needle to corner of smallest piece.

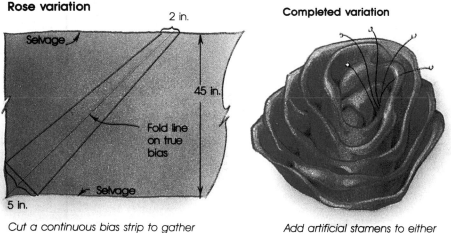

Rose variation

2 in.

Selvage

45 in.

Fold line on true bias

Selvage

5 in.

Cut a continuous bias strip to gather and roll into rose variation.

Completed variation

Add artificial stamens to either rose for realistic effect.

After completing one petal group and gathering petals for another, Carr begins drawing up the gathering threads on a small petal shape in the photo above. Below, she begins rolling the gathered petal into a flower center.

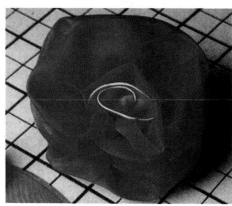

Carr mixes color and texture to get different effects. Yellow satin in the center of this magenta rose adds depth and interest.

Embellishing with Self-Fabric

Raveled and folded fabric shapes turn two dimensions into three

by Allyn Fiedler

a plain fabric does not have to be dull. You can transform it by sewing on scraps of the same material to give the surface texture and subtle contrast. After cutting and fraying these self-fabric scraps, you can fold, pleat, layer, or embellish them to create a variety of effects.

I began experimenting with appliquéd fabric shapes when I needed something to coordinate with a woven tapestry fabric that had a geometric design. I got the idea of stitching rectangles to a plain fabric to echo the shapes in the tapestry. The result was an interesting textured fabric that didn't really look like appliqué because it was all one color. The success of my first experiment encouraged me to try other projects with the same technique.

Getting started

A trip to the library to look at books on origami, napkin-folding, and geometric design can stimulate ideas for fabric shapes. You won't use many actual origami and napkin folding techniques because the multiple folds that give paper objects shape add too much bulk when used with fabric. But the books can suggest shapes and forms that you can adapt to a one- or two-layer piece of fabric. If you sketch these ideas with a few notes as you go along, you'll have ideas to experiment with when you get back to the sewing machine.

Long strips, rectangles, and squares are logical shapes to start with because it's easy to fray all their edges. That box of woven fabric scraps you've been keeping all these years

> ## Once you get started, you'll find that the design options are unlimited.

may yield some interesting materials to try. Wovens that ravel easily, such as linens, wools, heavy silks, and denims and other cottons, work the best.

For a session of experimenting, it's helpful to cut out a number of shapes at once. You can save time by cutting long strips first and removing threads along the long edges to create fringe. Then cut the strips into the desired squares or rectangles and fringe the remaining edges.

The photos on pp. 66-67 may give you some ideas. Try twisting, folding, pleating, pinching, or layering the shapes. Attaching the shapes with matching or contrasting threads, including metallic and variegated ones, will give different effects, especially when combined with decorative machine stitching. Beads can add an interesting accent, but make sure that they can be laundered or dry-cleaned just as your garment will be.

The threads you ravel from the edges can also become part of the design. They come in handy for attaching beads, stuffing shapes to add dimension, and stitching patterns on the fabric surface, as on the vest shown on the facing page.

For a wrinkled or puckered effect, experiment with a fabric that shrinks. Try sewing a few of the shapes onto the base fabric with the lengthwise grains perpendicular to each other. Wash and tumble dry to see if you like the puckered, checkerboard effect.

Planning for washability

A fringed edge will continue to ravel with agitation, especially on slippery or loosely woven fabrics; if you plan to wash or dry-clean the completed fabric or garment, finish all the raveled edges. On some designs, such as those at top on p. 66 and top right on p. 67, all the cut edges are zigzagged onto the base fabric just next to the fringe. But the other designs on pp. 66-67 rely on loose, frayed, unattached edges. For these, you'll need to finish the free edges before applying the shape to the fabric to prevent unwanted fraying after the pieces have been attached.

You can zigzag these loose edges either before or after raveling the fringe. To zigzag before raveling, it helps to pull a thread from the fabric where you want the fringe to stop, then stitch inside the line that you've created. If you zigzag after fraying, you may need to add a stabilizer under the shape to prevent the fringe from following the needle down through the hole in the throat plate of your sewing machine. There are several types of stabilizers that work for different fabrics, including water-soluble stabilizer (such as Solvy), stabilizers that crumble and brush off with the application

Transform a plain fabric into an exciting one by appliquéing self-fabric shapes. For the silk vest on the facing page, square shapes were fringed, folded, and stitched along the diagonals. The branches were sewn with the threads raveled from the shapes.

From *Threads* magazine (October 1994) 55:66-69

Photo by Susan Kahn; Vest pattern: Folkwear No. 152

A gallery of self-fabric embellishments

It's fun to experiment with self-fabric squares and rectangles to discover the variety of possible embellishment effects. You can rearrange shapes on the base fabric until you get a result you like. Zigzag stitching along all raveled edges will prevent further fraying.

Rectangles with windows are formed by fraying the outer edges, then pulling horizontal and vertical threads from inside each shape. Zigzagging secures the outside edges to the background fabric.

Each pinwheel motif is created from four smaller squares with raveled edges whose corners are overlapped. The squares are then stitched on the diagonal.

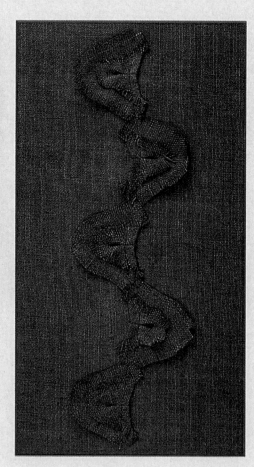

To form a row of arrows, first cut and fray a series of squares. Then, on each square, fold one point just short of the opposite point, make a pleat at the center of the folded side, and secure with a ³⁄₈-in.-long line of straight stitching. Arrange the arrows in alternating directions and stitch about ¼ in. from the fold.

The simple pinch shape is made by forming three small pleats on one edge and securing them with a bar tack. The samples are attached to the base fabric with a vertical line of stitching down the center.

Adding a fringe of beads to a shape is easy. String a group of beads onto a piece of the raveled thread, tie a few strings of beads together, and stitch this knot of beads onto the base fabric. Center a fringed rectangle over the knot and zigzag around the edges.

To make a fringed box, first cut and fray a square of fabric. Folding all the points to the center, stitch the shape to the base with one vertical and one horizontal row of stitching through the center of the folded sides. Metallic thread adds a highlight of color.

For a stylized bow, fold three pleats in the center of a rectangle, anchor them with a bar tack, and hand sew the shape to the base fabric using a long bead to secure it. Test to make sure the beads can be washed or cleaned by the same method as your garment.

of heat (such as Heat-Away), and tear-away stabilizers (such as the iron-on type called Totally Stable). Experimenting with scraps of fabric and stabilizer is the best way to determine which product will work best. For the delicate, non-washable silk in the vest on p. 65, I couldn't use a tear-away or dissolving stabilizer, but the brush-off stabilizer worked well.

You can also seal the edges with a fray-preventing product such as Fray Check, Aleene's Stop Fraying, or No-Fray. Be sure to test these products on the fabric because they may create a stiff edge or darken the fabric.

Creating a unique look

Once you get started, you'll find that the design options are unlimited. You can sew one shape across a garment, combine two techniques as I did on the vest, or mix several shapes, perhaps using one on each area of a patchwork garment. Depending on whether you want a random, overall texture or shapes that fall in specific locations on a garment, you can stitch shapes to the fabric yardage or to the cut garment sections. The amount of extra yardage you'll need for the shapes depends on how much testing you plan to do. An extra half-yard of fabric will go a long way.

Shirt or jacket yokes and pockets make good display areas for layered shapes. You may want to emphasize a sleeve by stitching a row of fabric shapes, such as the arrow design on the facing page, down the center sleeve. Or you might try accenting a garment front with pulled thread rectangles. Creating original fabric helps make a garment that's unique. ☐

Allyn Fiedler has been a Bernina educational consultant, a commodities stockbroker, a commercial real estate agent, and an art student. She is currently studying naturopathic medicine in Fountain Hills, AZ.

Leaf Printing on Fabric

Photosensitive dyes develop in sunlight

by Betty Auchard

A collection of flowers, leaves, and fern fronds coated with dye creates a delicate, realistic bouquet in soft tints when printed on a cotton shirt. On the silk scarf, a repeated leaf print softened with fine splatters of dye gives a muted allover effect. The transparent dye is permanent and leaves no stiffness on the fabric.

Photo by Susan Kahn

i print with anything that grows. Fresh or dried flowers, leaves, weeds, and even slices of fruits and vegetables—they all make wonderful prints when coated with dye and pressed to cloth. When exposed to sunlight, the dye that makes printing so easy for me, called Inkodye, develops into rich colors like those on the shirt shown on the facing page.

Working with Inkodye is fun, safe, and so easy that I've taught printing workshops to elementary school classes and to people with little art or craft experience. If you've tried painting fabric with an acrylic or fabric paint and found it messy to work with, slow to dry, or stiff on fabric, I recommend giving Inkodye a try. It leaves the surface soft, dries quickly, and cleans up with water.

Working with dyes

Inkodye is a photo-reactive fabric medium that comes in twelve hues or colors, plus brown, black, and clear. Mixing a color with clear lowers the intensity or concentration of the hue, which is very strong if used undiluted. Applying Inkodye to dry fabric results in a sharp image; on wet fabric it gives a blurred image.

Unlike many other dyes, Inkodye doesn't need steaming to set the color permanently. It sets best when exposed to strong sunlight.

If Inkodye is not sold in your local art supply store, you can order it from the manufacturer: Screen Process Supplies (530 MacDonald Ave., Richmond, CA 94801; 510-235-8330). Sizes begin at four ounces for $5.95. To get started, you'll probably want several colors in the smallest size, plus a larger amount of clear, which is less expensive. When you order, ask for an instruction sheet and a Material Safety Data Sheet, which explains that Inkodye contains no hazardous ingredients. Although Inkodye is nontoxic, inhaling the vapors can irritate the nose and throat. I recommend printing with adequate ventilation.

Selecting and preparing fabric

You can print with Inkodye on pure cotton, cotton blends, linen, silk, and rayon, although cotton is certainly the easiest. Since Inkodye is transparent when developed, it shows up best on a solid, light color. Before printing, launder the cloth to remove any dye-resistant finish, and press lightly. To prevent the dye from bleeding through to other layers, place fabric on plastic or line the inside of garments with a layer of plastic or cardboard before printing. Leave the barrier in place until the piece dries.

Starting to print

Before you print a shirt, try a color chart printed on cotton fabric (see "Making an Inkodye color chart" on p. 70). The information you gain will guide you in mixing and choosing colors for other projects.

Arranging leaves—When you're ready to begin printing a garment, first plan how you want to arrange the leaves into a design. Lay a few leaves on the cloth, as in the left-hand photo on p. 70, and experiment with different arrangements. You may want some, or all, of the leaves to overlap, as on the shirt on the facing page. If so, the first leaf you print will be in the foreground of the arrangement. Make a mental note of your design, but feel free to improvise as you go along.

Creating contrast for interest—To make an interesting print, contrasts of value (light and dark) are more important than contrasts of hue. Since each leaf may be left in place after printing, you'll have to remember where you've placed the values. Sometimes it's fun to combine colors "blind," or without planning. The results present some exciting surprises!

You may mix light values (the tints) in one of two ways: either in a dish or directly on the back of the leaf. To mix a light value on the leaf, spread a bit of clear Inkodye evenly over the back of the leaf with a brush, dab bits of one or more hues evenly over the clear, then brush them together for an even color.

Pressing and printing—After coating the leaf with Inkodye solution, you're ready to print. Press the leaf to the fabric, as shown in the right-hand photo on p. 70.

You can leave each leaf in place as you print, which masks the fabric under the leaf so the next printing occurs only on uncovered areas. Masking results in a layered effect, with some leaves and plants appearing to be behind others (see the print shown on the facing page). After each application of dye, spray the worktable with water and wipe dry.

Storing leaves

You don't have to use only fresh materials to make a print. I collect plants from my travels across the country, then store and reuse them.

After you've printed all parts of a design, remove the leaves, flowers, and twigs, and rinse them in cool water to remove the dye and refresh the plant materials. To reserve them for other prints, you can store most fresh leaves flat in a resealable plastic bag in the refrigerator for two or three weeks. I freeze the really sturdy specimens, then thaw and use them repeatedly. Don't reuse plant materials that become too brittle. ⇨

Preparing to print with Inkodye: An ideal worktable setup includes a pan of 2-in. shot glasses, labeled with permanent pen, to hold dye; a glass palette for mixing colors; and a tray for applying dye. You'll need a few flat brushes from ½ to 1 in. wide, a pan of water to clean the brushes, a spray bottle of water for table cleanup, and paper towels for drying. A bucket of flowers, buds, and leaves plus a jar of twigs and roots provides printing materials. If some leaves are shiny or waxy, spray them with a glass cleaner such as Windex and blot them dry. Brush a light coating of dye on the back of the leaf, where the veins are more pronounced.

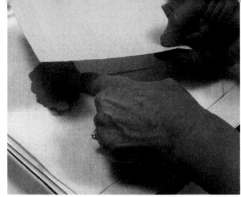

Deciding on an arrangement: Before beginning to print, move the leaves around until you're happy with the design. Keep in mind that the print will reverse the order of the arrangement; the yellow leaf print will appear to be in the foreground of the completed design. Once you begin printing, you can always alter the design as you go along.

To print: First pick up the coated leaf by the edges and place it dye side down on the fabric. Cover the leaf with a scrap of paper and press the entire surface and edges with your fingers. Avoid sliding your fingers while pressing, as this could force the dye beyond the edges or smear the print. Carefully lift the pressing paper and discard it.

Developing the print

It's fun to watch the Inkodye colors develop, especially for children. After printing is complete, lay your project on a clean surface in the sun. It takes 15 to 30 minutes in bright sunlight for complete development. In partly cloudy weather, it may take 90 minutes for colors to fully emerge. During winter, development can take several hours. Although the manufacturer suggests alternatives to sunlight for developing the colors, I find them so unsatisfactory that I prefer to wait for the sun.

As soon as the print is completely dry, it can be laundered. But first, you may wish to print a twig or two across the front of your design to pull the composition together. Develop and dry these additions to your design before laundering.

If you have no sunshine or it is too late in the day, set the printed project aside to dry, and place it in the sun at a later time. Don't be alarmed if the wet image is not visible when it dries, as it will still develop in the sun. However, I've found that I get stronger colors if I develop the print while the fabric is still damp.

If you wish to interrupt development to keep the colors soft and pastel, remove the print from the sunlight, let it dry in a dark place, and then launder to stop color development and remove excess dye. Launder the first time in a washing machine, not by hand, and dry on a setting appropriate for the fabric, or air dry.

Alternative design ideas

If a bouquet of overlapping plant materials seems too complex, you might want to begin with some of these ideas: You can print just around the neckline of a shirt for a collar or jewelry effect. For handsome stripes in a vertical, horizontal, or diagonal direction, print in the spaces between wide bands of masking tape. Or you can simply randomly scatter leaf prints over the surface, without making any attempt to overlap.

Making touch-ups

If you want to correct your design or hide an accidental drop of dye, leave the plastic liner in place, touch up the design, and then develop the finished print again. There are several techniques you can try for touching up: Using a toothbrush or fingernail brush to splatter a light color over the area covers some accidents and pulls the design together. Printing with additional plant materials can accomplish the same effect.

If you decide to make touch-ups with a brush and Inkodye, do it carefully, as this method is not very subtle and the result can look unrelated to the print. For a softer touch, I prefer to use transparent fabric pens, such as Niji Fabricolor markers and Marvy fabric pens (found at art-supply stores) for minor touch-up work. With pens, you can enhance the color and contrast, outline shapes, and add shadows to the final print. After using the pens, rub a slightly water dampened brush over the touched-up area to blend the edges and convert the "marker" look to a "dye" look. The result will be more subtle than using a brush with Inkodye.

To heat-set the fabric markers or pens, press with a hot iron for two to four minutes, moving the iron constantly to avoid scorching the fabric. ☐

Betty Auchard is a watercolorist and retired public secondary school art teacher. She and her husband Denny are working on a book about leaf printing on paper and fabric.

Before you print a garment, I suggest you make a labeled cloth color chart, which is a good way to explore the dye colors and learn how they change when mixed. See the photo of my chart on the facing page for ideas. One piece of fabric can hold a lot of information, and will serve as a useful reference when you begin printing.

Make a simple chart on white cotton fabric, painting a sample of each undiluted color, each color diluted with clear Inkodye (for tints), and each color mixed with black (for shades). It takes only a small quantity of an Inkodye hue mixed with clear to get a light tint. Try four brushfuls of clear to half a brushful of dye for a medium-light color, mixing them in a small dish or in a palette (see the photo on p. 68). Reverse the proportions when mixing shades. You'll need a smaller amount of black mixed with the dye color to get a darker shade.

Develop the chart in the sun, then label it with color names and measuring information using a permanent marker such as an extra fine point Sanford Sharpie. —B.A.

A piece of 20- by 27-in. white cotton fabric printed with Inkodye variations serves as a road map for future printing adventures. By mixing hues of Inkodye with clear, black, and with each other, you can produce a wide variety of colors and a useful reference tool to help you select colors while you print.

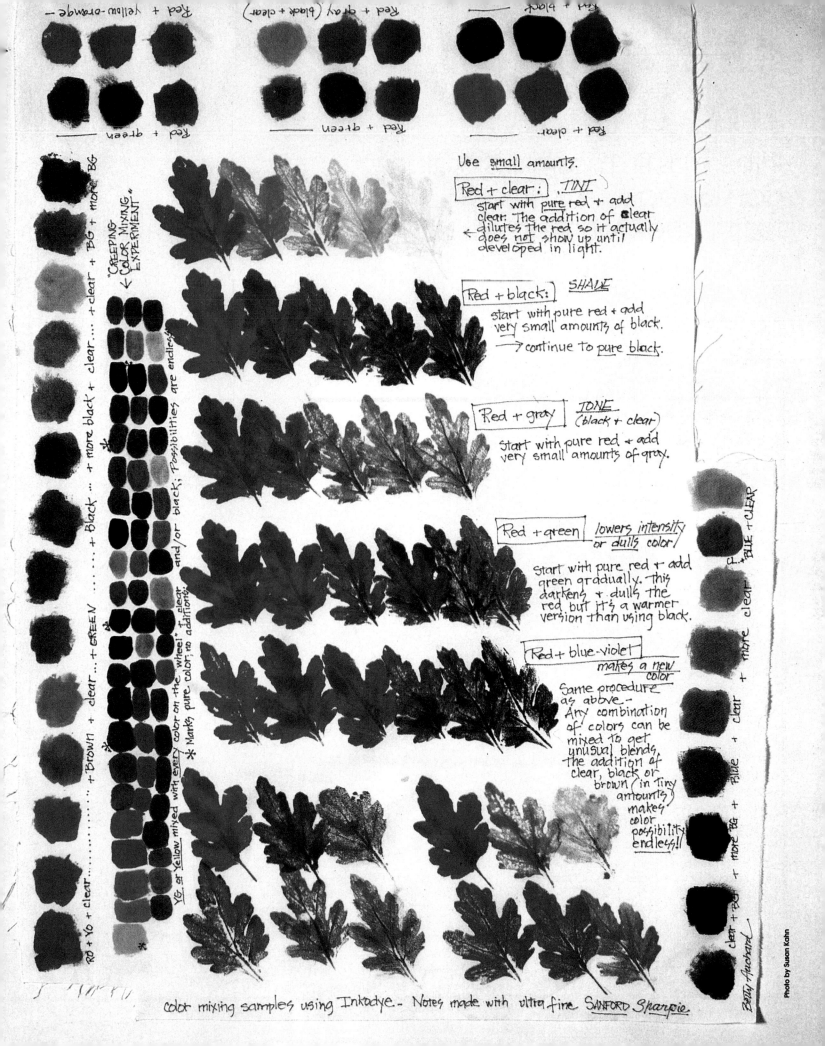

color mixing samples using Inkodye. — Notes made with ultra fine SANFORD Sharpie

Use small amounts.

Red + clear : TINT
start with pure red + add clear. The addition of clear dilutes the red so it actually does not show up until developed in light.

Red + black: SHADE
start with pure red + add very small amounts of black.
→ continue to pure black.

Red + gray TONE (black + clear)
Start with pure red + add very small amounts of gray.

Red + green lowers intensity or dulls color
Start with pure red + add green gradually. This darkens + dulls the red but it's a warmer version than using black.

Red + blue-violet makes a new color
Same procedure as above.—
Any combination of colors can be mixed to get unusual blends, the addition of clear, black or brown (in tiny amounts) makes color possibility endless!!

"CREEPING 'COLOR MIXING' EXPERIMENT"

RO + clear......... +Brown + clear...+GREEN ...... + Black ... + more black + clear... + clear + BG + more BG

RO + YO + clear.....

and/or black; Possibilities are endless
YR, or Yellow mixed with every color on the wheel.
* Marks, pure color; no additions.

BLUE + CLEAR
clear + more clear
clear + BG + Blue
clear + BG + more BG + CLEAR

Betty Auchard

Photo by Susan Kahn

Tambour Beading

Simple chain stitches worked with a hooked needle hold strands of beads to fabric

by Jan Bryant

When I was young, my mother had a friend who had beaded every gown that her daughter, an entertainer, wore on stage. I remember standing next to my mother's friend and leaning against the work table that held her beading frame, fascinated as she hand beaded the fabric for a dress. Much later, I met a designer who was looking for someone to help him bead dresses. He hired me and taught me how to bead with a tambour hook.

Over the years I've learned more about tambour beading and have developed the technique to the extent that I now teach the skill to others. To help you get started, I'll explain the basics: how to make a beading frame and stretch fabric onto it, and how to work a basic stitch—the chain stitch. You can practice making beginning and ending knots and beading on a piece of polyester chiffon that is stretched onto a homemade frame (see the instructions on p. 74). And when you're satisfied with your level of skill, you'll be ready to try your hand at creating a beaded garment.

For tambour beading, you work the chain stitches with your hook (see the inexpensive version on the facing page) on the wrong side of the work, anchoring the threaded beads on the right side. The advantage of tambour beading versus beading with a regular needle is that although it takes some time to master the hand motions, once these are learned, the beading proceeds much more quickly. The chain stitch is a locking stitch, which holds each bead firmly in place.

Beading on stretched fabric with a pointed hook, called tambour beading, is the most efficient technique for ambitious beaded projects like the black chiffon jacket with gold bugle beads at right. This article will get you started.

From *Threads* magazine (December 1992) 44:50-53

An inexpensive tambour hook and handle

A tambour beading needle needs a sharp point, unlike the blunter point of a tambour crochet hook. A shortened industrial machine-embroidery needle (No. 80, series 253M) (bottom of photo) makes an excellent tambour hook when inserted into a metal razor handle like the Excel USA, about $2 at art supply stores. Red nail polish painted on one quadrant of the handle vise marks the needle face position. Traditional wood (about $15) or metal handles also work, but the single screw tends to bend the needle. You can order a needle by mail from Jan Bryant. Send a check for $3 per needle and a self-addressed, stamped envelope to PO Box 8162, Los Angeles, CA 90008. The plastic tip cover that comes with the Excel handle is great for protecting the needle when it's not in use. To shorten the needle, break the shaft where it begins to thicken. Grip the threaded shaft with pliers, grasp the muslin-covered point and thin section, and snap the needle in two.

Beads

There are many different types of beads available, but whether they are the tubular bugle beads or circular seed beads, I like to use silver-lined, colored-glass beads because the silver makes the beads sparkle. Beads that are painted on the outside tend to lose their color, and the paint will rub off on your hands during beading.

For tambour hook beading, always buy beads in hanks, rather than loose. A hank has ten or more strings of beads tied together at the top in a simple knot that allows you to pull out one string of beads at a time. You're going to transfer the beads to your working thread, so don't remove the beads from the hank strings. If you are just getting started in beading, I recommend that you use No. 2 silver-lined bugle beads—a size that's easy to work with. These are the beads that I'm using in this article.

Fabric

While you can bead many different fabrics, polyester chiffon is one of the best fabrics to use for practice or for fancy garments. It is strong, and the holes made by the tambour needle do not spread (as they would in silk chiffon) and can be closed if you rub them with your fingernail. Chiffon in any color but black is trans-parent, so you can see what your hand underneath the fabric is doing. (Don't get black chiffon for your practice piece.) All that you need to try out the beading is a small rectangular piece, a half yard at most.

Transferring beads to the beading thread

Once you've made a frame and stretched your fabric, as shown in the drawings and photo on p. 74, you're ready to prepare the beads for tambour use. Place a spool of beading thread on the headless nail that you've hammered to the frame support or frame. I use 100 percent polyester sewing thread (Metrosene) for strength, in a color that matches the fabric. Never bead with the string the beads come on, because it is weak and will break.

Transfer a string of beads from the hank string to the beading thread, as shown in the drawing and photo at right. You can work with up to two strands of beads on your beading thread at a time, but never more. If you string more than two, the weight of the beads will cause the spool of thread to unwind.

Basic beading movement

For tambour beading, you hold the tambour needle in your dominant hand above

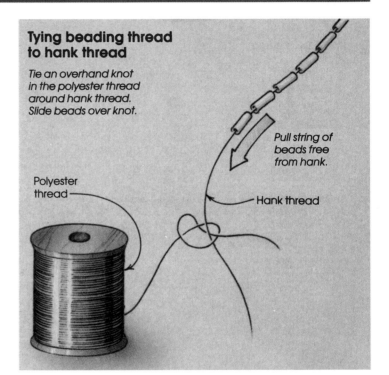

Tying beading thread to hank thread

Tie an overhand knot in the polyester thread around hank thread. Slide beads over knot.

Polyester thread

Pull string of beads free from hank.

Hank thread

Transfer a strand of beads to polyester sewing thread by carefully sliding the beads down the hank string, over the knot between the beading and hank string, and onto the poly beading thread, as author Jan Bryant does here. Moving slowly ensures that the knot stays in place and doesn't release to scatter beads all around the room.

Making a tambour beading frame and stretching fabric

These instructions will make a frame 25 by 38 in. All the supplies (below) are available at hardware and fabric stores. You'll need the help of another person to do the final tightening of the fabric.

Making stretcher bars

1. Staple a muslin strip to each 1-by-2.

Muslin

2. Fold over muslin and staple again. For 25-in. bars, staple a third time.

1-by-2

Pinning fabric to stretcher bars

1. Pin chiffon to muslin of longer bars, 1 in. from raw edges. Embed pin points in fabric.

2. Pin chiffon to shorter bars. Pin points stay above fabric.

3. Turn over 25-in. bars once, concealing pins; Turn under the 38-in. bars once. Clamp at each corner just to hold.

Muslin

38-in. bar

C-clamp

Polyester chiffon

25-in. bar

Glass-head pins

Do not pin muslin together at corners.

4. To stretch the fabric so it's drum tight, work one corner at a time. Grasp the ends of the bars and push the bars outward, as if closing a pair of gardening shears. A second person clamps the corner tightly with a C-clamp.

5. Now rest the frame across two saw horses or two table tops of equal height. Hammer a 2½-in. finishing nail (a headless nail) partway into the saw horse at the far left corner of the frame, or into the frame itself if you are resting the frame on tables. If you're left-handed, put the spool at the far right corner.

Supplies

- Four pieces of 1- by 2-in. clear pine: two 25 in. and two 38 in. long
- Unbleached muslin: two strips 6 by 25 in., two strips 6 by 38 in.
- Four 2-in. C-clamps
- Staple gun
- Glass-head quilting pins
- Rectangular piece of polyester chiffon, about 18 by 36 in.
- One 2½-in. finishing nail

the beading frame (see the photos on the facing page). Your other hand will be underneath the frame, handling the thread and the beads. Since I am right-handed, I've given instructions for holding the needle in the right hand. (If you are left-handed, reverse my instructions.)

The left (or less dominant) hand works the thread. The beading thread feeds up between the index and middle finger, over the index finger, and down between the index finger and the thumb. Hold both parts of the thread between your thumb and middle finger.

To work the hook, you'll need to pivot it, turning the face forward, backward, or sideways in relation to the design line. Except when starting and ending a line of stitching (at most, equal to the length of two hank strands of beads), you'll always insert the needle with the hook fac-

ing forward along the line; catch the thread with the hook turned sideways; and remove the needle with the hook facing backwards. Inserting the needle with the hook facing forward keeps the thread loop on the hook. Turning the hook sideways catches the thread securely. And when you remove the hook with the face backwards, you press the smooth shaft of the needle forward to open a hole in the fabric for the hook to slide smoothly from fabric and through the chain loop. The red mark that you've painted on the top of the handle (top photo, p. 73) tells you the direction that the hook faces when the needle is in your fabric, which is particularly useful when the fabric is opaque or black. The frame stays in one position and you rotate the hook as necessary.

You can work along a design line in whatever direction is comfortable. You can work a circle (see the drawing on the facing page) either clockwise or counterclockwise. However, for ease of movement, righties should always hook the thread to the left of the design line, lefties to the right.

Beginning a line of stitching

For practicing the basic maneuvers, draw a 6-in. line on the stretched chiffon, perpendicular to the long side of the frame, with a ruler and a dressmakers' pencil. Since you sit facing a long side of the frame, the line will be pointing away from you.

Knots that are tied only in the thread would eventually pull out of the fabric under stress, so I make a knot in the fabric by stitching twice over one stitch, as described below.

The first bead will hide the knot, so you'll work the knot slightly in from the start of the design line. Insert the needle on the design line about ¼ in. from the near end with the needle hook facing left (for righties); hook the thread. (Since there's no chain loop on the hook yet, you don't have to have the face turned forward.) Turn the needle face forward, press the back of the needle against the fabric (press towards yourself) to open the hole slightly, and slide the needle out. At the same time, pull down slightly on the thread with your left hand to maintain tension and prevent the thread from jumping off your hook as you lift your needle out of the fabric. There will be a loop of thread on the needle.

With the hook still facing forward, move forward about ¹⁄₁₆ in. and insert, still keeping tension on the thread with your left hand. Turn the hook sideways (left) and hook the thread. Turn the hook face backward, push the back of the needle against the fabric to open the hole (push away from yourself), and slide the needle out of the fabric and through the first loop. Keep the needle just above the fabric. Insert the needle into the first hole, hook the thread sideways, and remove the needle with the hook facing forward. Now pull the tail thread through the chain stitch and completely out of the fabric. To tighten the knot, pull the tail thread above the fabric and the spool thread underneath at the same time.

Basic beading

The three-step rhythm of the chain stitch, shown in the photo sequence at right, is: face the hook forward and insert; turn sideways and hook thread; turn backward, open hole, and remove hook.

The first bead always sits directly on top of the knot, hiding it from view. To place the bead, first insert your needle at the beginning of the design line with the hook facing sideways; hook the thread. Turn the hook forward, open the hole, and pull out the first chain stitch. With your left hand, slide a bead up and snug it to the fabric. Line the bead up with the line of stitching. Insert the needle (still facing forward), turn it sideways, and hook

the thread so the bead is now held in place. Turn the hook backwards, open the fabric, and pull the needle out. From here you continue with a regular chain stitch.

Ending knot

After you've stitched the last bead on your thread, you must make an ending knot by stitching across the design line between the last two beads. You'll need to use the face of a clock for reference. The end of the line is at twelve o'clock. Slide the last loop between the last two beads as shown in the lower right photo at right. Then use two and seven o'clock, starting at two. Pull the thread with your left hand to bring the needle down to the fabric. Insert the hook at two. Turn to seven, hook the thread, open the fabric, and remove the hook. Cross to just the other side of the design line at seven, insert the needle, turn to two, hook the thread, and remove the hook. Insert on the opposite side at two, turn to seven, hook the thread, and remove the hook.

To break the thread, first pull up the thread about 5 or 6 in. Hold the spool thread tightly in your left hand, slide the loop up over the rough base of your handle, and pull both loop and thread simultaneously until the loop thread breaks. This will also tighten the knot.

Only the start

The chain stitch can be used with beads other than bugle. You can use round beads, chaining between groups of beads, rather than after every bead. I often chain beads in parallel lines or side by side with a zigzag pattern of stitches. For a look at beautiful couture examples of beading, I recommend asking your library for the out-of-print *The Master Touch of Lesage* by Palmer White (1987; Chêne, France). □

Jan Bryant is a professional beader and beading instructor in Los Angeles.

Work chain stitches from the back

1. Insert needle with hook facing direction of stitching (in this case, down), while holding a bead snugged next to the underside of the fabric with your left hand. Note how the first bead sits on top of the beginning knot.

2. Turn the hook perpendicular to the stitching line (indicated by red mark) and hook the thread. Pull on the thread with your left hand underneath the fabric to keep the bead and thread from falling off the hook.

3. Turn hook away from the direction of stitching. Push fabric open with the smooth side of the needle shaft, and pull the hook out.

Starting an ending knot: Slide last loop between last two beads by pulling back on the needle and pulling the thread with the left hand.

How to turn the hook when beading curves

You can bead a circle clockwise or counterclockwise, whichever direction is the most comfortable. Righties always hook the thread to the left of the design line, lefties to the right. The frame stays stationary.

Here's how a rightie would work a circle clockwise.

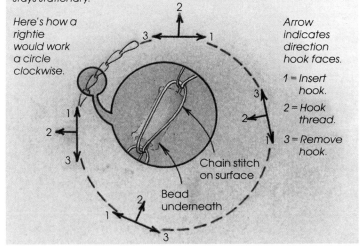

Arrow indicates direction hook faces.

1 = Insert hook.
2 = Hook thread.
3 = Remove hook.

Chain stitch on surface

Bead underneath

Illustrations by Clarke

A Thousand Points of Light

The basics of beading a garment with needle and thread

by Jeanne Leffingwell

Would you like to add some beaded pizzazz to a garment? As one who's been boggled by some pretty magnificent beading, I'm aware of the thousands of hours that have been spent perfecting the craft of attaching beads to fabric.

I've learned to bead by the seat of my pants. Constant tinkerer that I am, I have picked up many tips along the way. I offer these in a spirit of exploration and even reverence, in this technological age, for a craft that has never been successfully duplicated by machine.

Preliminary considerations

Stretching fabric flat and beading it prior to garment construction is easier, but there may be times you'd like to embellish a constructed garment. Sometimes the beading design simply doesn't crystallize until after you've finished the garment, or you might want to add beading to a purchased garment. This article will explain the basics of beading onto a previously constructed garment.

Preparation—Beading requires that the fabric be stretched and held taut by some means. Your setup can vary from stitching the fabric to a backing and stretching the backing on a frame, to simply holding the fabric smooth with one hand. For beading prior to garment construction, the garment pieces are usually cut with 1-in. to 2-in. seam allowances and basted to a backing cloth, which is then stretched on a frame. Occasionally, the fabric is stretched directly on a frame and beaded before the pieces are even cut out. Either way, after the beading is almost completed, the garment is constructed and any bare areas, such as over seamlines, are filled in.

Setup for a previously constructed garment requires more ingenuity. Using your hands may be the only option in tight places like sleeve edges, or where the garment cannot be laid out any flatter, but it is not necessarily the simplest. Setups are described in more detail under the discussions of the individual beading projects, which begin on p. 78.

Beading—There are two basic methods for securing the beads to the cloth using needle and thread (drawing, facing page). Stitch down each bead individually when the beads are scattered or when stretching the fabric on a frame would be undesirable. Whenever the thread must cross an inch or more on the underside to get from one beading spot to another, take a tiny stitch within the distance, ideally camouflaged next to another bead, to prevent long floats of thread.

Couching down a string of beads is faster but is suitable only when you want a line of beading. You must use a frame when couching; holding the fabric taut and couching at the same time would be very tricky.

There are in turn two variations of couching—a one-thread method and a two-thread method. Generally, the longer the line of beads being laid down, the more convenient it is to use the two-thread method; the shorter the line, the simpler it is to use the one-thread method. I make a couching stitch between every two to three seed beads and between every bugle bead. The photo on the facing page shows a sampling of commonly available beads.

Design—The weight of the beads will affect the drape of the cloth and, over time, the stability of the weave. The beads on the yellow blouse in the photo on p. 78 doubled the weight of the blouse—from 3 ounces to 6 ounces. Beading must be applied so its weight is balanced on the garment. This doesn't mean counting the beads or beading only in symmetrical patterns; it means that a concentration of beads in one area should be counterbalanced. Bead both sleeves, for example, not just one, or the back as well as the front of a blouse.

Fabrics—I like the ease of working on cotton, linen, and silk, but I have also worked on blends and synthetics and have found that with the right setup, nothing is impossible. Even a slinky 100% polyester, which normally fights a needle and causes thread-tension headaches, can be tamed if stretched properly.

To bead on chiffon or other lightweight fabrics, you can add underlining beneath the areas to be beaded and stitch through both layers; a second layer of the same fabric often works well. First bead samples using a few different underlinings.

Wait to work on a knit or any stretchy fabric until you've gotten enough experience with more stable fabrics to have a good sense of tension control. The trick to knits is stretching the fabric just taut enough so that the stitches won't cause it to pucker later, but not so taut that the threads and beads will pooch when the fabric is relaxed.

Some fabrics are more suitable than others for working without a frame. The raw silk bouclé blouse in the photo on p. 79 was ideal, as it had a certain "forgiveness" built into its texture—the fabric's slight elasticity and somewhat rough texture camouflaged small variations in tension.

Tools—Regular, good quality polyester or cotton sewing thread is quite adequate for

From *Threads* magazine (August 1990) 30:38-42

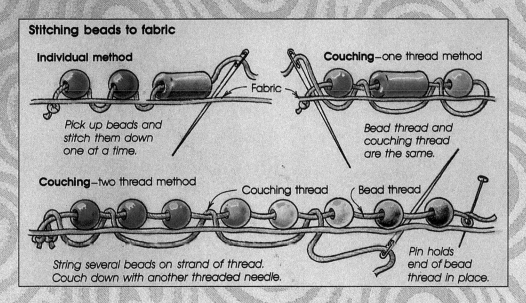

Stitching beads to fabric

Individual method

Fabric

Pick up beads and stitch them down one at a time.

Couching—one thread method

Bead thread and couching thread are the same.

Couching—two thread method

Couching thread

Bead thread

String several beads on strand of thread. Couch down with another threaded needle.

Pin holds end of bead thread in place.

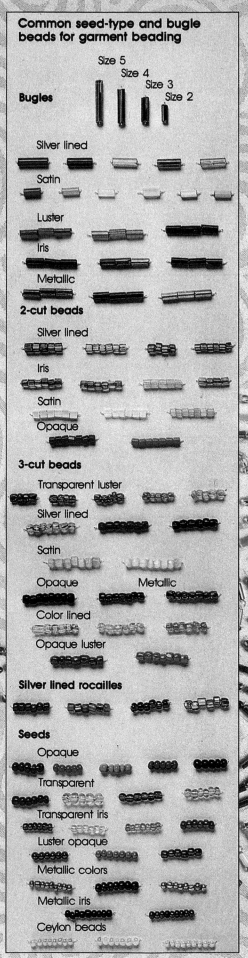

Common seed-type and bugle beads for garment beading

Bugles

Size 5
Size 4
Size 3
Size 2

Silver lined

Satin

Luster

Iris

Metallic

2-cut beads

Silver lined

Iris

Satin

Opaque

3-cut beads

Transparent luster

Silver lined

Satin

Opaque   Metallic

Color lined

Opaque luster

Silver lined rocailles

Seeds

Opaque

Transparent

Transparent iris

Luster opaque

Metallic colors

Metallic iris

Ceylon beads

---

most garment beading, although silk is stronger. I don't recommend either the thinner serger threads, which are difficult to work with, or nylon thread, which can melt when ironed. Match thread color to the background fabric, except in certain instances (for example, with transparent beads) where you should use the thread color that gives you the best overall affect.

I use a relatively short length of thread—never more than 28 in. to 30 in. long, as I have found that the extra time spent in more frequent waxing and threading is always less than the time spent untangling knots or unwrapping threads from around other beads. Even more important to me is the reduction in wear and tear on my stitching arm and shoulder. The longer the thread, the wider and more sweeping the motions required to pull it through the cloth with each stitch—no small consideration when you're planning to attach a few hundred or thousand beads to a garment.

I use a single strand of thread, waxed with pure beeswax. Waxing strengthens the thread and discourages fraying and tangling, and it usually helps with threading, too. My method of threading involves anchoring the cleanly snipped thread end close between my thumbnail and the pad of my index finger on one hand and slipping the needle eye down over the thread. My assistant uses tweezers.

Beading needles are thinner than regular sewing needles and generally longer. There are two kinds—sharps and longer ones that are simply called beading needles. Both kinds come in different sizes; match the needle to the beads you will be using, and make sure you have some needles that, when threaded, will pass through your smallest-holed beads. For sewing beads individually you can use the shorter needles. When couching lines of beads, a longer needle enables you to pick up more

beads at a time.

Since all needles eventually get metal fatigue or the eye slots get skinnier from use, keep a good supply on hand.

Whenever possible, and in particular when you are couching down lines of the same bead, pick up beads directly from the shank on which they come. Hold them in place with your fingers while you pull the shank thread back and out. Pick up loose beads with the needle held at a low angle.

Cull any questionable beads (too-small holes, broken edges, and so on) as you work. Percentages of imperfect beads vary with bead type, but you'll usually find some. There is no time-waster like a bad bugle cutting the thread after it's been stitched down.

Learn to work ambidextrously. Seriously—switch hands. In the long run learning to do all the motions with either hand will help you to stay aware of your alignment and balance.

Leave 5-in. or longer tails on top when you near the end of your thread (if you leave them underneath you'll have a real mess soon), and pin them out of the way when necessary as you work. When the beading is finished, or at the end of each session if you prefer, thread each tail again, this time with a regular sewing or crewel needle (aahhh, what large eyes). Bring the thread to the back and knot securely.

Work in good lighting. Please don't waste your eyes. Take advantage of daylight and work near a window whenever you possibly can. Train yourself to gaze outside regularly to give your eyes a rest.

Don't bead with your shoulders hunched up or with your neck and back shaped like a teapot spout. Get your work to a comfortable height. Lower your chair or block up the table. Put another block under your feet to see if that's more comfortable.

Take breaks frequently. Don't be a victim

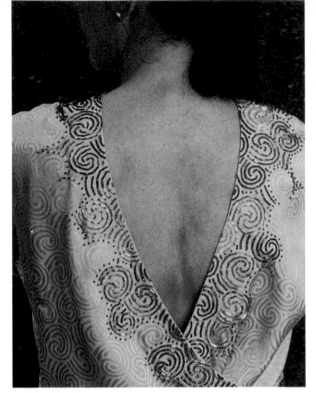

Leffingwell derived the beading design for this blouse from the pattern woven into the fabric. (Photo by Susan Kahn) After basting the blouse to a muslin backing (slipstitching along neck edge), Leffingwell carefully cuts away the muslin from beneath the areas that will be beaded (top right). With the blouse secured to the muslin, Leffingwell stitches the top and bottom edges of the muslin to cloth strips attached to the bars of her tabletop embroidery frame (center right). Leffingwell couches down a line of beads (bottom right).

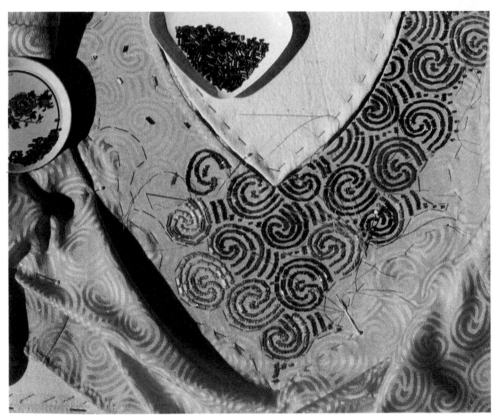

After stitching a line of beads, Leffingwell pins the thread tails out of the way. Later she will rethread each tail with a sewing needle, bring it to the back side, and knot it. The individually stitched beads are guides to the colors she plans to use for that area.

of the endless "I'll just finish this last little bit" syndrome. Beading is a most tedious form of handwork, and as any victim who has suffered this syndrome's aching shoulders and twitching eyeballs knows, the whole body is the instrument. And a good worker takes care of all her tools.

Caring for beaded garments—Some garments made of washable fabric can be handwashed *if* all the beads on it are colorfast. To check the colorfastness of a type of bead before attaching them to the garment, shake a few in a small jar containing warm water, drain, and let dry, then compare them to their unrinsed mates. Beads that are not colorfast will be noticeably paler than those that weren't rinsed. Certain pinks and purples and almost all colorlined beads are notoriously not colorfast.

Most beaded garments can be cleaned by a good drycleaner, but be wary. I wouldn't put my time into beading a garment that because of tight-fitting armholes, for example, would need frequent cleaning.

If a beaded garment needs ironing, either steam it, without actually touching the fabric or the beads, or use a thick pressing cloth. Glass beads can get hot enough to harm certain fabrics or thread.

Working out projects

To illustrate in more detail the different setup and beading procedures, I will explain how I handled three quite different beading projects.

Yellow blouse—For the beading design on the yellow blouse shown at left I chose to use a motif woven in the fabric and to couch swirling lines of bugles and seed beads. I first basted in a general outline of the area that I planned to bead. I determined that I would need three positionings in a frame in order to work each section flat: the front and each side of the back. The area that I could lay out flat at one time also determined what size frame I would need, as I wanted to reposition the blouse in the frame as few times as possible. An adjustable rectangular embroidery frame with a stand, designed for tabletop use, was perfect.

I ripped a piece of muslin for the base cloth, large enough to attach to the frame all around. After smoothing out the first beading section and pinning it to the muslin, I slipstitched the neck edge to the muslin, then basted the other sides of the fabric to the muslin approximately ½ in. outside the outline stitches. On the back I cut away the muslin from underneath the beading area, just inside the basting stitches and about ⅝ in. inside the slipstitches at the neck edge, as shown in the top right photo at left. Because I planned to bead right up to the neck, I folded and basted this ⅝ in. of muslin back out of the way. Finally, I machine-basted a pair of cotton straps with eyelet holes in them to the sides of the muslin. I made these reusable devices for lacing the muslin to the frame to save time.

To attach everything to the frame, I first whipstitched the top and bottom edges to a strip of cloth stapled to the bars of the frame, as in the middle right photo at left. I laced string through the eyelet holes and around the sides of the frame.

When I bead with many different colors, deciding which color to put where can be painstaking. I frequently use what I call my "dot system," which allows me to make a whole group of decisions at once and takes the place of a more formal plan or cartoon. I baste down one bead as a guide for each color area. I remove them as I fill in the areas.

Except for the outline of purple beads, stitched down singly, all of the bead lines on this top are couched down. When couching down bead lines, leave a little air between the beads to prevent the lines from scrunching up once the fabric is off the frame and relaxed. This happens because the tiny couching stitches, which are so many little anchors along the line, themselves take up some space. A line of beads that's 2 in. to 3 in. long on the string will actually cover an extra ⅛ in. to ¼ in. once it's stitched down.

Couching is easier if both hands are free as much as possible for making the stitches. To help keep in place the line of beads you're couching without actually holding it, put a straight pin at the far end and wrap the bead thread around it temporarily.

When I'd finished beading the first section, I removed everything from the frame and took out the basting stitches to free the garment from the muslin backing. After taking all the thread ends to the backside and knotting them, I was ready to rip a new piece of muslin and repeat the entire process for the second section. This isn't as daunting as it may sound. Seeing that first sparkling section keeps up the momentum.

Teal blouse – For the teal blouse shown in the photo at right, I used what I call a stream-of-consciousness style for both the design and the stitching. This was an already constructed garment and I beaded without a frame, holding the fabric smooth with one hand while stitching beads singly with the other. To give myself an idea of what area I hoped to cover, I sometimes basted in a few lines or drew them with an embroidery marking pen that fades out completely in a couple of days, but otherwise I simply beaded as I went along. I laid out the garment frequently as I worked,

Sources

Retail

Western Trading Post
Box 9070
Denver, CO
80209-0070
(303) 777-7752
Sample cards available.

Garden of Beadin'
Box 1535
Redway, CA
95560
(707) 943-3829
Catalog $2.

Wapenish Trading Post
702 West Ninth St.
Wapato, WA 98951

(509) 877-4554
Send samples or order by name.

Wholesale
Minimum order is usually ½ kilo or 1 kilo per bead type or color. Send samples or order by name.

Elliot, Greene & Co., Inc.
37 West 37th St.
New York, NY
10018
(212) 391-9075

Har-Man Importing Corp.
16 West 37th St.
New York, NY
10018
(212) 947-1440

For the beading on this blouse Leffingwell stitched each bead individually, simply holding the fabric taut with one hand.

Leffingwell wanted a freestyle look for the beading on this raw silk bouclé blouse. She picked beads at random from her box of loose green-mix beads. (Photo by Susan Kahn)

These beaded lapels are removable, allowing the garment to be washed as usual. The beading design was inspired by the print on the fabric. (Photo by Paul Rainer)

Making a removable beaded lapel

⬤ Broadcloth backing
⬤ Beaded fabric
○ Fixed lapel of jumpsuit

Turn under and stitch edges of broadcloth to beaded lapel fabric.

Snap

Beaded lapel wraps around fixed lapel on jumpsuit and is secured in back by snaps.

and I tried it on now and then to see how the beading was progressing.

I limited the color scheme to shades of green and turquoise. I used bugles in different lengths (3mm, 4mm, and 5mm) and different types of seed beads: square- and round-holed rocailles, 3-cuts, opaques, luster opaques, metallics, irises, and ceylons, mostly size 10/0 and 11/0. I avoided beads I knew were not colorfast so that I could wash the garment, but otherwise I just dipped methodically from my loose green-mix beads. For this kind of work I pour a small quantity of beads onto a flat white plate with low sides. Plastic airline dishes and some frozen-entree plates work well.

I deliberately applied the beads in the simplest scatter-beading manner, one by one. I did not want to couch down lines of beads because I was not using a frame.

The hardest thing about beading without a frame is getting the knack of how much tension to use in the stitching. Too little tension and some beads may droop, just asking to be snagged; too much tension (the more common problem) and the fabric will pucker or otherwise be pulled out of alignment. The magic touch, even and smooth, comes with practice.

Since this was a finished garment and the design rather freely executed, there is nothing to keep me from adding more beads if some area begins to look bald or deprived, or simply if the spirit to bead moves me again.

Black and white jumpsuit—For the jumpsuit shown in the photo above my assistant Gael Bukvich beaded removable lapels that I had designed to snap to the fixed lapels on the garment. An advantage of being able to remove the beadwork is that the garment can be laundered as usual; also it can be worn with or without the beaded lapels. Collars, cuffs, epaulets, and pockets are other possible locations for beading. Gael did the beading on the lapels during construction of the jumpsuit, but you could add a similar detail to a finished garment.

I cut out the fabric pieces, leaving at least 1-in. seam allowances on all sides. I machine-basted each piece to a larger square of muslin approximately ½ in. outside the seam line of the lapel. I cut away the muslin just inside this basting line from underneath the area to be beaded.

Together we stretched the piece on a simple wooden stretcher frame meant for canvas, using pushpins at 2-in. intervals. We started pinning at the centers of opposite sides, keeping grainlines even.

For beading, Gael placed the frame over the edge of a table and weighted it on the far side with the head of a hammer so both her hands would be free to handle the beads and thread. A C-clamp would have provided a little more stability, but this set-up was quicker to rearrange.

The print on the cloth, which includes zigzags, circles, dots, spirals, curving and straight lines, and stick figures, had suggest-ed to me the beading design and stitches. Gael beaded parallel concentric circles of seed beads, radiating zigzags and bands of bugles, straight and curving lines in alternating colors, bugle "stars," and individual seed "dots." She used #12 beading needles, both long and short, and both a one-thread and a two-thread couching method.

After I took the finished pieces off the stretcher and the beaded fabric off the muslin backing, I trimmed the seam allowances to ½ in. To back each removable beaded lapel and finish off its raw edges, I applied a piece of lightweight cotton broadcloth, cut ¾ in. larger all around, behind it. I turned under the two straight edges of the broadcloth backing, then turned them under again and wrapped them around the raw edges of the beaded piece, as shown in the drawing above. I stitched these edges down, creating bound and finished edges for the removable beaded lapels. I bound the curved neck edge with a bias strip of the backing fabric.

The bound edges of the beaded lapel wrap around the edges of the fixed lapel and snap to the back of the fixed lapel and to the inside of the garment, where they aren't visible even when the jumpsuit is worn without the beaded lapels. ☐

Jeanne Leffingwell designs large sculptures in beads for architectural spaces as well as beaded garments from her home in Moscow, ID. (Photos by author except where noted)

Buttons from Thread

Crochet is quick and elegant

by Nancy Nehring

Searching for buttons in a fabric store is not my favorite activity. One day, after a wasted trip trying to find buttons for a silk jacquard blouse, I went home and crocheted them instead. In two hours I had the buttons I wanted.

Crocheted buttons make up quickly and easily. Besides buttons, these small projects readily become interesting earrings, pendants, brooches, and cuff links. By changing threads and stitches, you can create an infinite variety of colors and textures, like those in the photo at left and on p. 83. Some require no more knowledge of crochet than a single stitch. You need only three items to get started—thread, a steel crochet hook, and a button mold or stuffing. You crochet the button top separately, working more tightly than for normal crochet so the button will be firm and keep its shape, then finish the button on the mold. Since buttons are small, compared to a project like a sweater, the work goes quickly, even

Delicate buttons crocheted in silk thread can perfectly match a silk jacquard blouse or an evening jacket cuff. All a button takes is a crochet hook, thread or yarn, and a mold. For instructions for the metallic circle button on the cuff, see p. 83.

with fine thread. After practicing, you should be able to complete most buttons in ½ to ¾ hour.

If possible, crochet a button before making the buttonholes on your garment. Crochet may add substantially to the size of the button mold, even using the finest threads.

If you choose a thread size different from the one suggested in the pattern, adjust by using a different size mold to fit the crochet, or change the number of rounds on the top and side to fit your mold.

Threads

You can make wonderful buttons from many different types of threads and yarns. Generally, the smaller the button, the finer the thread you will use. Cotton crochet thread, ranging in size from 100 (finest) to 10 (thickest), is a good choice for your first buttons. I like size 80, called tatting thread, which comes in a wide range of colors.

Silk buttonhole twist makes a button with a beautiful luster. Rayon machine-embroidery threads, such as Sulky and Altazar, are available in many colors at fabric stores and produce a silklike button. Linen thread for lace making produces strong, durable buttons, although the colors are limited.

Yarn can be used to make matching buttons for knitted garments. Separate yarn plies and work with a single ply to make a delicate, durable button. Try unraveling thread from fabric to make matching buttons. Don't be afraid to experiment with unusual threads. See "Supplies" on the facing page for a source of many threads.

Crochet hooks

Using a steel hook for fine work is no different than crocheting with a larger aluminum or plastic hook, except that the work comes out smaller. Steel hook sizes range from 14 (smallest) to 00 (largest). Select the size to match your thread, which should just fill the groove of the hook. I use a size 13 or 14 crochet hook with size 80 tatting cotton.

Molds and stuffing for shaping

Most buttons require a mold or stuffing for support. When choosing a button mold, you should select a material that can be cleaned the same way as the garment, or crochet button covers and remove before cleaning. Or you can make

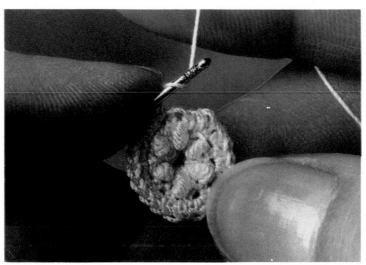
Make the baby bullion button with a size 13 steel crochet hook and size 50 crochet cotton. After crocheting the bullions, or knobs, over a small metal washer, complete the button in simple single crochet.

removable buttons, described in "Attaching the button" at right.

Self-covered button blanks are my favorite choice of mold for buttons. Available in many sizes in notions departments, they are made in two pieces: a top, and a back that has a shank in the center. Use larger sizes for pendants and brooches: remove the shank and attach a cord or use hot glue to add a pin back. Self-covered earring molds have a post attached to the back instead of a shank. Button molds, earring molds, and removable button covers are available in the notions area of fabric stores.

Crochet is too thick to fit between the top and back of the mold. Instead, cover the mold according to its package directions with a thin fabric such as batiste or broadcloth in a coordinating color, since this fabric will show through the holes in the crochet. Then cover the entire button with crochet, forming a cap over the covered mold.

The **plastic or brass rings** used for café and balloon curtains can also support crochet. For small buttons, use a knitting stitch count marker or flat washer.

You can make round, ball-like buttons with only a dense center of **polyester batting** for support. Cut equal-size circles of batting so all your buttons match. **Beads,** purchased **buttons** with or without shanks, **bottle caps,** or **champagne corks** with the stem cut off can all be used to give shape to your buttons. Cover these molds by cutting a circle of fabric just larger than twice the diameter plus the depth. Fold the fabric over the mold and whipstitch the back together, or gather the outer edge to the center back of the mold and sew.

Anatomy of a button

The crochet work for a button can be divided into three sections: the top, the side, and the back. The top may be flat or domed, and is usually crocheted in a circle from the center outward like a doily. On each round, the number of total stitches increases by eight to twelve stitches, depending on the type of stitch (single, double, or treble). A round of treble crochets may require more than eight extra stitches to keep the work flat. For a domed mold, add fewer stitches in the outer rounds so the top curves to fit the mold.

The side rows cover the button depth and contain equal numbers of stitches, giving depth without increasing the diameter. Some buttons with a sharp edge have no side section. Once you've crocheted the side of any of these buttons, you're ready to slip the mold into the cover or stuff it firmly.

Last, you close the back to keep the crochet on the mold. One method is to decrease two stitches into one continually until you reach the center back. Another method is to tie off the crochet, leaving a yard-long thread tail, and sew with the tail in a star pattern across the back (12 o'clock to 6 o'clock, 1 o'clock to 7 o'clock, etc.) to hold the crochet on the mold.

Attaching the button

Attach the finished button to the garment using one of three methods: For a button with a shank, simply sew the button to the garment. For a button without a shank, sew it to the garment by catching a few threads at the center back of the button, or add a shank with a few loops of thread covered with buttonhole stitches (see *Threads* No. 46, p. 16).

Here's my trick for making a button that's removable for cleaning: pair the crocheted button with a small, flat, two-hole plastic button back to back, making a short shank if the button does not have one. Make buttonholes on both sides of the garment to fit the smaller plastic button. Simply unbutton to remove for laundering. This method works for cuff links too, and you can use use crocheted buttons on both sides. □

Nancy Nehring lives in Sunnyvale, CA, and is working on a book about making buttons of crochet, needle lace, embroidery, and braid.

Crocheting the finishing touches

You can create wonderful buttons for your garments by following the patterns below. Practice first with a larger yarn and hook to familiarize yourself with the stitches.

Notes

Find stitch instructions for chain (ch), single crochet (sc), half double crochet (hdc), double crochet (dc), treble (tr), and double treble (dtr), in Threads No. 46, pp. 16-18.

An asterisk (*) means that the chain of 1, 2, or 3 sts at the beginning of a round counts as the first sc or dc of that round.

When you see [to], repeat the stitch(es) between brackets.

Supplies

Susan Bates Steelite hooks, Candlelight metallic yarn, size 50 crochet cotton, size 80 tatting thread, and Kanagawa silk threads are available by mail from the Craft Gallery (PO Box 145, Swampscott, MA 01907; 508-744-2334).

Circle Button

This easy button is worked entirely in single crochet in closed circles. (See gold button on p. 81.)

- Candlelight gold metallic yarn
- Size 9 steel crochet hook
- 1-in. (size 45) half-round button mold

Note: This style button can be worked as a circle (gold button) or a spiral (white buttons on p. 81), depending on whether you close each round with a slip stitch or not, respectively.

Top:

Rnd 1: Ch 4, slip stitch (sl st) 1st to last loop to form a ring.
Rnd 2: Ch 2*. 7 sc in ring. Sl st to join.
Rnd 3: Ch 1*. 2 sc in each sc of prev rnd. Sl st to join.
Rnds 4, 5, 6: Ch 2*. 1 sc in 1st and 2 sc in next sc of prev rnd; repeat around. Sl st to join.

Side:

Rnd 7: Ch 2*. Sc around. Sl st to join. Insert mold.

Back:

Rnd 8: Ch 1, sc in every other sc of prev rnd. Tie off; anchor back by sewing in a star design, as described on facing page.

Cluster Button

A group of five double crochet stitches forms each cluster, or petal.

- No. 80 red tatting thread
- Size 14 steel crochet hook
- 9/16 in. (size 24) half-round button mold

To dc 5 together (dc5tog): [Wrap yarn once over hook (yo), insert hook, draw a loop through, yo, draw through 2 loops]; rep 4 times in same space. Yo and pull through all 6 loops on hook.

Top:

Rnd 1: Ch 8 and join with sl st to form a ring.
Rnd 2, form inner ring of petals: Ch 2*. 8 [dc5tog, ch 2] in circle. Sl st to join top of last puff to 1st.
Rnd 3, create a ring of paired petals: Sl st into 1st ch 2 loop. Ch 2*. 2 [dc5tog, ch 2] in each ch 2 loop around. Sl st in top of 1st puff to join.

Side:

Rnd 4: Sl st into 1st ch 2 loop. Ch 2*. 3 dc in each ch 2 loop around. Sl st to join.
Rnd 5: Ch 2*. Dc in each dc around. Sl st to join. Insert mold.

Back:

Rnd 6: Ch 1. Sc in every other st around, continue to center of back. Tie off.

Daisy Button

This button makes a wonderful cuff link on a crisp white shirt. Single crochet in circles forms the center; each curved petal is formed by a sequence of nine stitches from short to tall, and back to short.

- No. 80 yellow and No. 80 white tatting thread
- Size 14 steel crochet hook
- 9/16 in. (size 24) half-round button mold

Top:

Rnd 1: With yellow thread, ch 4, sl st to form ring.
Rnd 2: Ch 2*. 8 sc in ring, sl st to join.
Rnd 3: Ch 2*. 2 sc in each sc of prev rnd. Sl st to join.
Rnds 4, 5, 6: Ch 2*. Sc in 1st st and 2 sc in next st of prev rnd; repeat around. Sl st to join.

Side:

Rnd 7: Ch 3*. Dc in each sc of prev rnd. Sl st to join.
Rnd 8: Ch 2*. Sc in each dc of prev rnd around. Sl st to join. Insert mold.

Back:

Rnd 9: Ch 2, sc in every other sc of prev rnd; repeat to center of back. Tie off.

Petals:

Rnd 1: Attach white thread around bar of dc with sl st, [ch 5, sc around fourth dc] repeat around (use third or fifth dc to make it come out even if necessary). Sc around 1st dc to join.
Rnd 2: Sc, hdc, dc, tr, dtr, tr, dc, hdc, sc in each loop around. Sl st to join. Tie off.

Baby Bullion Button

Form center bullions over a flat metal ring. For firm, tight bullions, use a hook with an untapered shank, such as the Susan Bates Steelite hook.

- No. 50 cotton crochet thread (I used white and dyed it after completion. You can also use Kanagawa No. 16 silk thread, available in 211 colors.)
- Size 13 Susan Bates Steelite crochet hook
- 4mm flat washer with 2mm inside diameter, from hobby shop (called a 2mm washer, Dubro No. 2107)
- 7/16 in. (size 18) half-round button mold

To make a bullion: Start with a single loop of thread on hook. Yo 7 times between loop and hook. Take up thread through center of ring; holding all 8 loops (7 yo plus original loop) on shank of hook at bottom so they don't slip; pull loop on hook through 8 loops on shank with twisting motion, or pick loops off one at a time. Sc over ring to hold bullion in place.

Top:

Rnd 1: Attach thread to washer with a slip knot and pull up a loop. Make 6 bullions with sc between, as described above. Join with sl st.
Rnd 2: Ch 1. Sc in top of each bullion and in each sc between, for 12 sts. Join.
Rnd 3: Ch 1*. 2 sc in each sc of prev rnd. Join.
Rnds 4 & 5: Ch 1*. Sc around. Join.

Side:

Rnds 6 and 7: Repeat rnd 4, 5. Insert mold.

Back:

Rnd 8: Sc in every other sc of prev rnd to center back. Tie off. —N.N.

Needle-Lace Buttons

Using a needle and thread, you can weave the perfect garment finish

by Nancy Nehring

needle-lace buttons are like tiny weaving projects. They are made by first laying down a base thread, and then weaving or wrapping a decorative thread design around the base. Without spending a lot of time and effort, you can create these small, richly textured button masterpieces that will add a special look to your garments.

I've adapted several elegant designs from buttons found on vintage garments. For some styles, the base wraps in two directions, forming an X pattern, while for others the base consists of many evenly spaced wraps around the button mold, in what I call the clock pattern (shown in the box below). The design is either woven around the base threads with a needle or sim-

ply wrapped around the mold, using the base threads to anchor the wraps. Complete instructions for three button styles begin below.

Selecting materials

The materials required for needle-lace buttons are basic: All you need is a mold (which will remain inside the button), some thread, and a needle, plus fabric or thread to cover the mold if the lace design is open, so you won't see the mold.

Molds—Needle-lace buttons require rigid molds that will hold up to wrapping without deforming. I use bone or wooden disk beads (shown on the facing page), which have a hole in the center to allow the thread to pass from front to back; they're available from bead suppliers.

If the button pattern is lacy or open like the flag button (shown at the bottom of the photo on the facing page), you'll need to cover the mold with fabric or thread, so the mold won't be visible. To cover a mold with fabric, cut a fabric circle a little bigger than twice the diameter of the mold. Run a gathering stitch by hand or machine near the edge, insert the mold, pull the gathering stitches tight, and tie off the thread. The fabric will form a lump at the center back, which you can use as a shank to attach the button to the clothing, or you can make a thread shank (as discussed in *Threads* No. 50, p. 20).

To cover the mold with thread, I like to use flat silk thread such as Kreinik's Soie Platte or Japanese embroidery silk (for sources, see

"Supplies" on p. 86). Wrap the mold evenly in the clock pattern until it's fully covered.

Threads—You can experiment with many different types of fine thread to make needle-lace buttons; generally the larger the button you want, the thicker the thread it will require. Some of my favorite threads include a lustrous, tightly twisted silk cord from Germany (Griffin No. 4, made for stringing beads), silk buttonhole twist, ordinary crochet cotton, and fine linen threads.

Balancing the design—Buttons look best if their size is in proportion to the garment, so you may need a larger or smaller button than the examples shown here for your garment. You can adjust the three variables of thread

---

Just one of these intricately textured needle-lace buttons, each shown next to its mold or ring, makes the perfect finishing touch at the neck of a jacket or shirt, or as a brooch. Or make a complete set for a special garment. From the top, the sea urchin button uses crochet cotton and just one easy stitch; at center, the smooth Leek button is made from fine linen thread, while the checkerboard Leek variation at center left is of silk buttonhole twist; at center right, the small star shirtwaist button uses crochet cotton wrapped around a ring and is finished with buttonhole stitches; at bottom, the woven flag button is wrapped in a high-twist silk cord made for stringing beads.

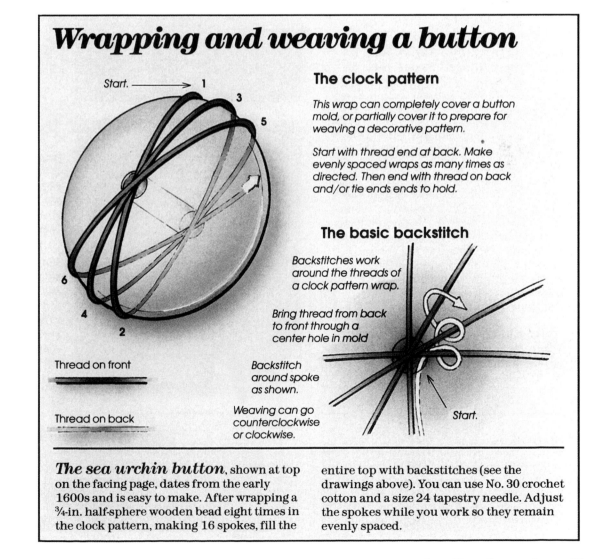

Wrapping and weaving a button

The clock pattern

This wrap can completely cover a button mold, or partially cover it to prepare for weaving a decorative pattern.

Start with thread end at back. Make evenly spaced wraps as many times as directed. Then end with thread on back and/or tie ends ends to hold.

Start. → 1
3
5
6
4
2

Thread on front

Thread on back

The basic backstitch

Backstitches work around the threads of a clock pattern wrap.

Bring thread from back to front through a center hole in mold

Backstitch around spoke as shown.

Weaving can go counterclockwise or clockwise.

Start.

***The sea urchin button**, shown at top on the facing page, dates from the early 1600s and is easy to make. After wrapping a ¾-in. half-sphere wooden bead eight times in the clock pattern, making 16 spokes, fill the

entire top with backstitches (see the drawings above). You can use No. 30 crochet cotton and a size 24 tapestry needle. Adjust the spokes while you work so they remain evenly spaced.

Woven flag button

Named for the tiny flags that wave on each spoke (see bottom button on p. 84), this button dates from the 1860s, when it was available ready-made on cards or as a kit, with the mold already wrapped in flat silk. You can adjust the pattern to fit your thread size and mold by varying the number of rounds of backstitch pattern at the center or the number of wraps in the flags.

Mold: 1-in. wood domed knife-edge bead
Threads: Soie Platte (flat silk) to cover mold (a 10-meter reel covers two buttons) and Griffin No. 4 silk beading cord (three cards will make two buttons)
No. 26 tapestry needle

1 **Cover the mold:** Hold one end of flat silk thread at center back, leaving a tail for tieing, and wrap silk in the clock pattern (as shown on p. 84), with each wrap just touching the last, until the mold is fully covered. Cut the thread, leaving a 6-in. tail, and thread onto the tapestry needle. To anchor wraps, go from back to front through center hole, over the area where the wraps cross at the top center, and down through the hole. Repeat, crossing the top center at 90 degrees to the first stitch, forming a tiny X. Tie the ends in a square knot at the back, and trim close to knot.

2 **Base:** Cut off and discard the wire needle that comes attached to the silk beading cord, then thread the tapestry needle (flatten the cord to insert; you may need a needle threader). Tie the cord at center back, leaving a 1-in. tail. Wrap the button in the clock pattern so that the thread crosses the top of the button six times, making 12 evenly spaced spokes for weaving, and anchor as for flat silk above, with one stitch. Tie a square knot at the center back, but don't cut.

3 **Design:** Bring the thread up through the hole to center front, and weave seven rounds of backstitch as shown at lower right on p. 85.

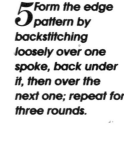

4 (Shown at left.) Weave the flags by backstitching over two spokes four times; end with a backstitch on a single spoke, then repeat using the second spoke and the next empty one. For the last section, squeeze the needle under the first four wraps.

5 Form the edge pattern by backstitching loosely over one spoke, back under it, then over the next one; repeat for three rounds.

6 To hold the last set of backstitches between each pair of spokes in place, run the needle under a few strands of flat silk (on back of button), under and over the three backstitches, then pull tight to form a V. Repeat between each pair of spokes. Tie the thread at the center back. —*N.N.*

Supplies

You can order Kreinik's flat embroidery silk from The Daisy Chain (PO Box 1258, Parkersburg, WV 26102; 304-428-9500), silk bead cord from General Bead (637 Minna St., San Francisco, CA 94103; 415-621-8187), and crochet cotton and linen threads from Lacis (2982 Adeline St., Berkeley, CA 94703; 510-843-7178). You'll often find wooden bead molds in bins of assorted beads at local bead and craft stores, or you can order them from Nancy Nehring (see address on the facing page). Or use your imagination and try plastic buttons as molds, or make your own molds from wood, mat board, stiff plastic, or wine corks; attach nonwashable buttons with button pins (available on button racks at local stores).

Leek button

This button dates from the early 1800s, when it was produced by a cottage industry near Leek, England, and often used to fasten men's vests and coats. The basic Leek button (instructions below) is shown at center on p. 84, with a checkerboard variation just to the left. The trickier variation is made by weaving the top in a pattern, over and under every five threads.

Mold: ¾-in. bone or wood disk bead mold

Thread: 35/2 to 50/2 linen thread (One 40-yd. card will make several buttons.)

No. 24 tapestry needle

The Leek pattern is formed entirely by wrapping. You start with an X wrap to anchor the subsequent covering wrap.

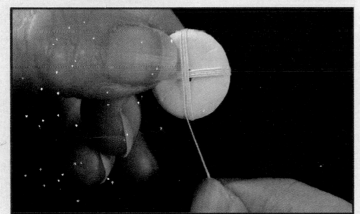

2 Beginning the cover: Wrapping just beside the X threads so that they anchor the new thread, follow the numbers from 1 to 8: across the top, across the bottom, up and down at right, up and down at left. The thread always crosses diagonally in the back.

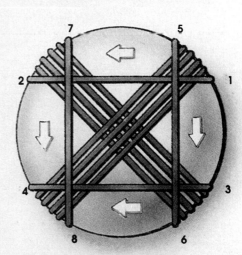

1 Wrapping the X: Holding the thread tail at the center back of the mold, wrap four times around the center of the mold. Turn the mold using the tail to anchor the threads, and wrap again four times at a right angle to the first set.

3 Repeat the sequence, laying the new thread close to the previous wrap and moving toward the center. If the thread begins to slip as you near the center, cut the thread about 6 ft. long, thread the needle, and run it under previous rounds on the back of the button to hold.

4 When you reach the center, thread will cover the entire mold. Adjust the threads with the point of the needle if necessary. From the back, take one stitch up through the hole in the mold, over the last four wraps, and down to the back. Tie the ends to finish.

thickness, mold size, and pattern until they look just right. Usually I pick a mold size and thread that are appropriate for my garment, and then adjust the pattern so that the finished lace just fills the mold, without crowding. On most of the patterns, the number of base wraps can be increased or decreased to suit the thread and button size, and you can adjust the weaving pattern by increasing or decreasing the number of wraps each pattern section makes over the base, or by eliminating or creating one or more pattern sections. Before I begin the actual garment buttons, I always weave a few test buttons to make sure that the mold, thread, and pattern will work together, and to perfect my technique so all the garment buttons will look alike. □

Nancy Nehring is writing a book about button making. (For her article on crocheted buttons, see pp. 81-83.) Molds and complete kits for many of the buttons shown in this article are available from her at PO Box 2892, Sunnyvale, CA 94087.

The Uncommon Closure

How to button up with everything but an ordinary button

by Lois Ericson

Unusual closures are my trademark. In fact, an ordinary button is normally my last choice for a fastener on a garment or belt. For me, the closure isn't an afterthought when I'm designing a wearable. I make it an integral part of the whole design. When I have a garment in mind to make, I think about how to fit together the fabric and the closure within the silhouette to make each seem perfect for the other. To put it in one word, what I'm looking for when I design are relationships.

Sometimes I start with an idea, a problem to solve, a way to "get the look." Usually this comes from a photo, from a picture of a building, from nature, or from some other image. Often I'll cut a basic garment shape away from the center of a sheet of black paper and then move the sheet over an intriguing photo from a book or magazine until I've isolated a few patterns within the opening that suggest internal lines for the garment. The cutout makes it easy for me to see the patterns in the photo without getting bogged down in what the picture is actually of. Then I start looking for the perfect fabric and closure for the shapes that have inspired me.

Sometimes it's a wonderful object looking for the right setting that gets me started. Even the shapes on the fastener-to-be can be the point of departure for the design of the whole garment. I can repeat the outer shape of the object or its surface design by stitching lines, by using faced shapes, or by stenciling. Maybe the photo image or the object has a texture that some fabric manipulating could repeat. If the object is heavy, maybe it needs to be put on a quilted wearable. Even if it's rather ordinary, I think about ways in which I can make the application more interesting. I try to analyze what it is about the item that I relate to besides the color. Look carefully at the collection of objects that you have; maybe something that I've done in the photos on the next few pages will give you a new idea for using them. Try designing around those objects, looking for new possibilities. Avoid doing things the same old way merely because it's easier.

Buttons—Most sewers have a collection of buttons, so that's a good place to start looking for uncommon closures. If the buttons are flat ones with holes through them, notice if the backs have more texture or better color. If they do, use them with the reverse side up. Try nonmatching buttons that have perhaps the same color, material, or size. Are they the wrong color? Then, use acrylic paint to coat them or to create a design that relates to the print on the fabric. If the buttons have large holes, consider using a braid or cord instead of thread to hold them in place. Tack the center of a 6-in. piece of braid to the garment, slide the braid through the holes in the button, and tie it to secure it. Or slide several buttons onto the braid, positioning them where desired and sewing the braid in place.

Notice how things work. Remember the manila envelopes with the two buttons and string to wrap them together in a figure eight? That's an idea worth translating into a closure. My jacket closure in the top photo on p. 92 fastens the same way—with two Art Deco buttons and covered cording.

When there is only one wonderful button, and the overall design of the garment is going to be rather plain, consider echoing the shape of the button, or shapes within it, by stenciling or stamping a design from the button onto the fabric, as in the photo at top left, p. 93. A stencil can easily be cut from an acetate page protector with scissors or a blade-type cutter. Fabric paint can be applied through the stencil opening with a fine sponge or a brush. Stamps can also be made with sponge rubber glued to a block of wood. For either method, use the fabric paint sparingly for the best results.

Buttonholes—I rarely use machine-made buttonholes. Instead, I use a faced hole (similar to, but simpler than, a bound buttonhole) or cording sewn along the edge of the garment with spaces left to accommodate the buttons. If the button is so unusually large that any buttonhole looks too big or so irregular in shape that it is difficult to button, I attach a covered cording to the opposite side and wrap the cord around the button to close the garment.

To make a faced buttonhole, cut a facing 1 in. or more larger than the desired buttonhole. On the facing, draw the shape of the hole you want. Place the facing in the appropriate place on the garment's right side and machine-stitch along the line you drew. Cut through both layers inside the stitching and clip to the corners, as you'd do to make a piped pocket opening. Then turn the facing through and press it. You can turn under the edges of the facing and tack them on by hand on the wrong side, or you can conceal them under the garment lining or facing. On the vest at bottom center, p. 93, I put in the buttonholes after facing the entire vest, so I stitched through all layers and tacked the edges to the garment facing.

Covered cording sewn on the edge of the garment, with spaces left for buttons, subtly conceals buttonholes. When the garment isn't buttoned, the slits are barely visible, and the cording appears to be trim on the finished edge. Cover cording with bias fabric to match your garment, as described in the drawings on p. 90, or use commercial cording available in a matching or contrasting color. Sew the buttons on where you want them. Then, on the finished edge of the wearable, handsew the cording to the edge of the right side, leaving slits slightly larger than the buttons and in line with them. For added interest, make a few overhand knots in the cording as you apply it to the edge of the garment, remembering to allow extra length in the cording for the knots. The knots also make turning corners easy.

Beyond the button—To create an unusual closure, I try to look beyond what an object is called to see it for what it is, just as I do with the photos I use for inspiration. Labels seem to narrow down the item's potential for use. Naturally, it's great to have a large collection of treasures from which to choose. I have a cabinet (photo, p. 90) full

Lois Ericson's short jacket is made perfect by her careful play with covered cording, silver beads, and decorative knotting. Not at all by accident, the large beads are also working buttons.

Ericson's earthly treasure—the ultimate button hoard, in the perfect cabinet.

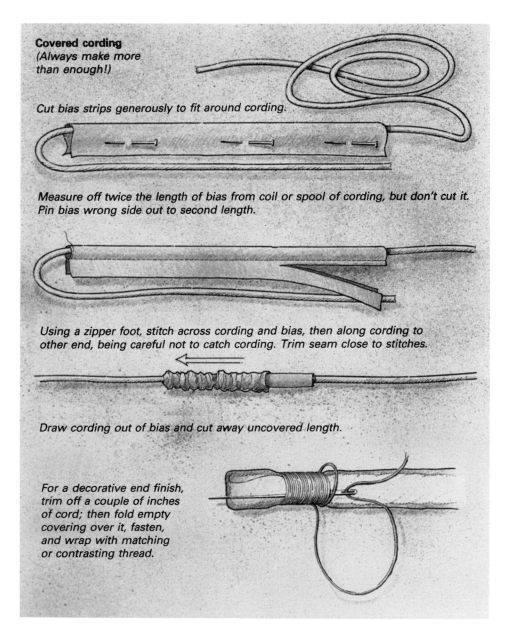

Covered cording
(Always make more than enough!)

Cut bias strips generously to fit around cording.

Measure off twice the length of bias from coil or spool of cording, but don't cut it. Pin bias wrong side out to second length.

Using a zipper foot, stitch across cording and bias, then along cording to other end, being careful not to catch cording. Trim seam close to stitches.

Draw cording out of bias and cut away uncovered length.

For a decorative end finish, trim off a couple of inches of cord; then fold empty covering over it, fasten, and wrap with matching or contrasting thread.

of pieces purchased from antique and second-hand stores or given to me by friends. I've also found interesting items in stores that sell hardware, boating supplies, plastic supplies, fishing tackle, and electrical equipment. The fact is that almost anything can serve as a closure.

Bracelets make great fasteners and are easy to find in various materials and sizes. Sectioned or linked bracelets can be divided, and the clasp can be used as the fastener. To accentuate a pocket, cuff, or other design feature, consider sewing on the rest of the pieces as well. One-piece band bracelets of metal, bone, or wood can easily be used as closures combined with fabric ties.

Frogs—Once you start knotting covered cord, it's a short step to making frogs (formerly called frogging), the decorative knotting that I used in the jacket on p. 89. Many materials lend themselves to corded types of fasteners: braids, trims, rounded leather cords, velvet ribbons, thin ropes, etc. Round shoelaces come in many lengths and can be dyed easily. Your frog design could be just a series of loops stitched in place, any one of which could serve as the button loop. Small objects or beads can be strung or sewn onto the cording. I like to add frogs to long, unknotted pieces of cording, which I use to outline, emphasize, or create design lines on the garment as a whole.

The easiest way to start is to make single, isolated knots (see drawings, p. 91). You can begin by improvising knots and spirals, or you can refer to books on knotting for more tried-and-true designs. Celtic and Viking design books are filled with intricate knotwork interlacings, as are many old illuminated manuscripts. Nature photography of intertwined vines, grasses, and seaweed is a great source for more freewheeling ideas. Knots and frogs can be made to repeat prints or textures from your fabric.

You can draw your designs on cardboard and then pin one end of the cord at a good starting place, holding the loops in place as you go with little stitches underneath. The loose ends can be tucked out of sight and tacked down later. Buttons can be beads or toggles strung onto the cording, or they can be formed from knots in the cording, but two facing loops can form a closure without buttons, as shown on p. 91.

This is just a small sampling of the closures that are possible. When the flow of ideas is combined with a wonderful object, there is usually only one solution that is just perfect. Have fun sewing! ⇨

Lois Ericson is the author of four books on designing with textiles, including Design and Sew It Yourself: A Workbook for Creative Clothing *(1983), which contains many other interesting ideas for garment-making and embellishing. All four books are available from Ericson at Box 1680, Tahoe City, CA 95730.*

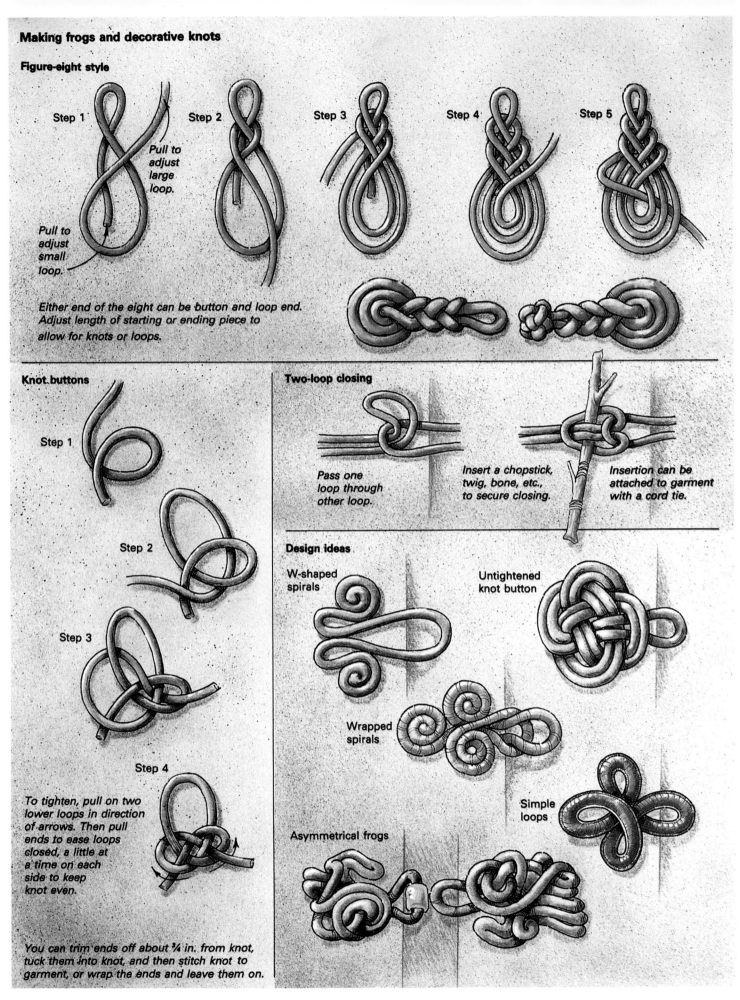

Making frogs and decorative knots

Figure-eight style

Step 1

Pull to adjust small loop.

Pull to adjust large loop.

Step 2

Step 3

Step 4

Step 5

Either end of the eight can be button and loop end. Adjust length of starting or ending piece to allow for knots or loops.

Knot buttons

Step 1

Step 2

Step 3

Step 4

To tighten, pull on two lower loops in direction of arrows. Then pull ends to ease loops closed, a little at a time on each side to keep knot even.

You can trim ends off about ¼ in. from knot, tuck them into knot, and then stitch knot to garment, or wrap the ends and leave them on.

Two-loop closing

Pass one loop through other loop.

Insert a chopstick, twig, bone, etc., to secure closing.

Insertion can be attached to garment with a cord tie.

Design ideas

W-shaped spirals

Untightened knot button

Wrapped spirals

Simple loops

Asymmetrical frogs

A gallery of closures

Lois Ericson approaches each of her garment designs as an exercise in relationships—how to find the best combination of all the elements: the fabric, the cut, the colors, the textures, and the embellishments. The crowning touch is almost invariably an inventive and well-chosen closure, like the closures that complete the extraordinary garments shown here. Common to many of Ericson's closures is the use of fabric structures—tubes, flaps, and straps—instead of thread alone, to hold objects in place and together. A manila envelope's figure-eight clasp inspired the two-button and cord-tie closure on the cropped jacket above. Band bracelets and rings of all kinds are ideal for fabric-tie closures, as on the jacket at left. Bias strips of striped fabric accent the sleeves and hold onto the antique ivory beads that close the jacket Ericson wears at right.

Rubber stampings homemade with fabric paint on the garment fabric above mimic the design of the antique button. A covered cording closure and tiny buttons don't distract from the strong pattern at right. A gold-filled watch fob ties together the linear elements of the taupe ribbed-and-quilted silk fabric below.

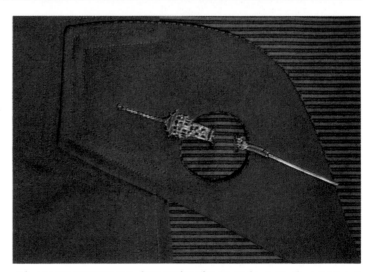

Instead of buttons and buttonholes, the vest above has two carnelian rings tied down with fabric strips that fit into faced slots. A faced flap, with a faced circle cut from it, is centered over a pair of ma-

chine-made buttonholes, into which fits an Oriental hair ornament. Additional pairs of buttonholes, out of sight beneath the flap, provide adjustability (above, right). ☐

Index

Look for these and other *Threads* books at your local bookstore
or sewing retailer.

Couture Sewing Techniques
Shirtmaking
Fit and Fabric
Fitting Your Figure
Great Sewn Clothes
Jackets, Coats and Suits
Techniques for Casual Clothes
Beyond the Pattern: Great Sewing Techniques for Clothing
The New Quilt 1
The New Quilt 2
Quilts and Quilting
Great Quilting Techniques
Designing Knitwear
Fair Isle Knitting
Hand-Manipulated Stitches for Machine Knitters
Knitting Lace
Knitting Counterpanes
Swedish Sweaters
Hand-Knitting Techniques
Knitting Around the World
Colorful Knitwear Design
Celebrating the Stitch
Stitchery and Needle Lace
Hooking Rugs

For a catalog of the complete line of *Threads* books and videos,
write to The Taunton Press, P.O. Box 5506, Newtown, CT 06470-5506.